THE POWER OF A
PRAYING PARENT

Stormie Omartian

D0189559

HARVEST HOUSE PUBLISHERS
Eugene, Oregon 97402

All Scripture quotations in this book are taken from the New King James Version, Copyright © 1979, 1980, 1982 by Thomas Nelson, Inc., Publishers. Used by permission.

Cover by Koechel Peterson & Associates, Minneapolis, Minnesota

THE POWER OF A PRAYING PARENT

Copyright © 1995 by Harvest House Publishers
Eugene, Oregon 97402

Library of Congress Cataloging-in-Publication Data
Omartian, Stormie
    The power of a praying parent / by Stormie Omartian
        p. cm.
    ISBN 1-56507-354-1
    1. Prayer—Christianity.   2. Parents—Prayer-books and devotions—English.   3. Devotional Calendars.   I. Title.
    BV220.053   1995
    248.3'2'0240431—dc20   95-8627
                                                                                        CIP

All rights reserved. No portion of this book may be reproduced in any form without the written permission of the Publisher.

Printed in the United States of America

                    00   01   02   03   04   / BC /   19   18   17   16

Contents

Acknowledgments

With special thanks:

To my daughter, Amanda, and my son, Christopher, for filling my life with joy and giving me so much to pray about.

To my husband, Michael, for his willingness to spend countless hours with me over the last twenty years covering our children in prayer.

To my secretary, Susan Martinez, for being a gifted and valuable helper, encourager, comforter, sister, and friend.

To my friend and fellow praying parent, David Hazard, for encouraging me to write this book.

To my brilliant editor-in-chief and dear sister in the Lord, Eileen Mason, for her vision for this book, her heart for concerned parents everywhere, and for freely sharing the richness of her sweet and godly spirit.

To my gifted editors, Betty Fletcher and Judith Markham, for all their invaluable input.

To my Harvest House family, Bob Hawkins, Sr., Bob Hawkins, Jr., Bill Jensen, Julie McKinney, and LaRae Weikert, for faithfully using their enormous talents for God's glory and for their dedication to helping me and other authors bring hope and help to all who need it.

To my prayer partners, Susan Martinez, Roz Thompson, and Jan Williamson, for the many hours of prayer time they've invested in this project, in my children, and in my life.

To my long-distance prayer partners, Debra Goldstone, Pamela Hart, and Lisa Welchel Cauble, for not forgetting me when I moved to Tennessee and for deeming this project valuable enough to commit to prayer.

To my spiritual father and pastor for twenty-three years, Pastor Jack Hayford, for teaching me how to pray.

To Pastor Dale and Joan Evrist, for reminding me that my treasure can only be found in the face of God.

To my spiritually adopted son, John Kendrick, for letting me be his mom on earth ever since his first mom went to heaven.

To my housekeeper, Thelma Peña Lopez, for seventeen years of faithful service and for showing me that a mother's heart has no language barrier.

Foreword

My mom has been a great mother to me. She encourages me and tries to help me with everything. I am very thankful for her prayers and love. She prays for me daily and I think that is one of the reasons I make it through school and life. Her prayers have made a difference to me, and because of them, I am alive on this earth. One time her prayers made a big and wonderful change in my life that I never imagined could possibly happen. At my school, I had a classmate who was very mean and I never wanted to go near her because she scared me. When I told my mom, she decided we should pray together for this girl. I thought that was a good idea and so we prayed nearly every day until school was out and through the summer too. The following school year, a miracle happened and that girl changed completely, and she became one of my best friends. It affected my life and it was one of the greatest things that ever happened to me.

Mom's praying worked. It doesn't always work, but even when our prayers aren't answered right away, just praying or being prayed for makes me feel better. I am thankful for God and my mother. Thank you, Mom.

Amanda Omartian (13 years old)

Well, I must say that I have truly been blessed with a couple of parents who are very loving and caring, very understanding, and, yes, even occasionally funny. But of the many wonderful qualities my parents possess, the one that I respect most is their persistence in prayer for me and my sister and our everyday lives. If I were to tell you how much their prayers have meant to me and made a difference in my life, I would probably end up writing more than my mother. But since you probably did not pick up this book to read my writings, I will pinpoint the most memorable time in my life where having praying parents really paid off.

Throughout all of my eighteen years, both of my parents have constantly been in prayer for my safety. While growing up in the "peaceful" city of Los Angeles, those prayers kept me shielded from danger. I clearly remember one particular time during my freshman year in high school when God protected me in a serious auto accident. Two other boys and I were driving to school one morning and were not wearing seat belts when we collided nearly head-on with another car turning left in the intersection. One of my friends was severely injured when he went through the windshield, and the other boy hit the steering wheel with his face. I was in the back seat and ended up with only a minor injury to my lower back. In a situation where everyone could have died, God put His protection over the car and spared all three of us. It was at that point in my life when I realized just how important prayer is, and I gained a clearer perspective of God's awesome power in the midst of disastrous situations.

I am eternally grateful to my parents for their persistence in praying over my life. It has truly made a difference in not only sparing me from danger, but also keeping me on the right path as an honest, moral person.

I guess now that I am eighteen years old, the prayers of my parents will probably change somewhat. I suspect they may be praying that I will hurry up and get married so they can have the house to themselves.

Christopher Omartian (18 years old)

Pour out your heart like water
before the face of the Lord.

Lift your hands toward Him for the
life of your young children.

LAMENTATIONS 2:19

CHAPTER ONE

Becoming a Praying Parent

It's the best of jobs. It's the most difficult of jobs. It can bring you the greatest joy. It can cause the greatest pain. There is nothing as fulfilling and exhilarating. There's nothing so depleting and exhausting. No area of your life can make you feel more like a success when everything is going well. No area of your life can make you feel more like a failure when things go wrong.

PARENTING!

The word itself can bring contradictory emotions to the surface. We try to do the best we can raising our children. Then, just when we think we've got the parenting terrain all figured out, we suddenly find ourselves in new territory again as each new age and stage presents another set of challenges. Sometimes we sail through smoothly. Sometimes we encounter tempests and tidal waves. Sometimes we get so tired that we just want to give up—let the storm take us where it will.

But I have good news. We don't have to be tossed and turned by these winds of change. *Our children's lives don't ever have to be left to chance.*

We don't have to pace the floor anxiously, biting our nails, gnawing our knuckles, dreading the terrible twos or torturous teens. We don't have to live in fear of what each new phase of development may bring, what dangers might be lurking behind every corner. Nor do we have to be perfect parents. We can start right now—this very minute, in fact—making a positive difference in our child's future. It's never too early and never too late. It doesn't matter if the child is three days old and perfect, or thirty years old and going through a third divorce because of an alcohol problem. At every stage of their lives our children need and will greatly benefit from our prayers. The key is not trying to do it all by ourselves all at once, but rather turning to the expert parent of all time—our Father God—for help. Then, taking one step at a time, we must cover every detail of our child's life in prayer. There is great *power* in doing that, far beyond what most people imagine. In fact, don't ever underestimate the power of a praying parent.

I didn't have the best role model for parenting because I was raised by a mother who was mentally ill and very abusive. I wrote about that abuse and my miraculous recovery from its effects in my book *Stormie* (Harvest House Publishers). I also related how having my first child, our son Christopher, caused me to realize that I had the potential in me to be an abusive parent. I discovered that without God we are destined to repeat the mistakes of our past and to mimic what we've observed. A scene from childhood can flash across the screen of your mind and play itself out on the stage of your life in a moment of weakness—before you even realize what has happened. It may occur so quickly that you feel powerless to control it, and it can make you do and say destructive things to your children. This becomes compounded by the guilt that inevitably takes root and grows to often paralyzing proportions. Thankfully I had good counseling and support and was able to overcome this problem before any damage happened to my child, but many people have not been so fortunate.

Because I was painfully aware that I didn't have a positive parenting experience to imitate, I was nervous and anxious when my first child was born. I feared I would do to him what had been done to me. I read every book available on the subject of parenting and attended each Christian child-rearing seminar I could find. I tried to do my best with all this good and helpful information, but it was never enough. I had countless agonizing concerns for my son's social, spiritual, emotional, and mental growth, but most compelling of all, I feared that something bad might happen to him. Kidnapping, drowning, disfiguring accidents, irreparable injuries, diseases, sexual molestation, abuse, rape, or death all played across my mind as possibilities for his future. As much as I tried not to be an overreacting parent, every newspaper, magazine article, or TV newscast on crime made me more concerned for his welfare. Plus we lived in Los Angeles, a city where crime was rampant. It was more than I could handle.

One day in prayer I cried out to God, saying, "Lord, this is too much for me. I can't keep a twenty-four-hours-a-day, moment-by-moment watch on my son. How can I ever have peace?"

Over the next few weeks the Lord spoke to my heart about entrusting Christopher to Him. My husband and I had dedicated our son to God in a church service, but God wanted more than that. He wanted us to continue giving Christopher to Him on a daily basis. This didn't mean that we would now abdicate all responsibility as parents. Rather, we would declare ourselves to be in full partnership with God. *He* would shoulder the heaviness of the burden and provide wisdom, power, protection, and ability far beyond ourselves. We would do *our* job to discipline, teach, nurture, and "train up a child in the way he should go" knowing that "when he is old, he will not depart from it" (Proverbs 22:6). We were to depend on God to enable us to raise our child properly, and He would see to it that our child's life was blessed.

An important part of our job was to keep the details of our child's life covered in prayer. In doing this, I learned to identify every concern, fear, worry, or possible scenario that came into my mind as a prompting by the Holy Spirit to pray for that particular thing. As I covered Christopher in prayer and released him into God's hands, God released my mind from that particular concern. This doesn't mean that once I prayed for something I never prayed about it again, but at least for a time I was relieved of the burden. When it surfaced again, I prayed about it again. God didn't promise that nothing bad would *ever* happen to my child, but praying released the power of God to work in his life, and I could enjoy more peace in the process.

I also learned that I should not try to force my own will on my child in prayer. This only leads to frustration and disappointment for all concerned. You know the kind of prayer I mean, because we're all prone to it: "God, I pray that Christopher will grow up and marry my best friend's daughter." *(Her parents would be great in-laws.)* Or, "Lord, let Amanda get accepted at this school." *(Then I can feel better about myself.)* Of course we may never consciously acknowledge the words in parentheses, but they are there in the back of our mind, subtly inspiring us to impose our will in God's ear. I have found it's better to pray more along the lines of "Lord, show me how to pray for this child. Help me to raise him Your way, and may Your will be done in his life."

By the time our daughter, Amanda, was born four and a half years after Christopher, God had taught me what it means to pray in great depth and to really intercede for my child's life. Over the next twelve years God answered my prayers in many wonderful ways, and today I see the results.

My husband and I recognize the hand of God on our children's lives, and they readily acknowledge it as well. For it's the power of God that penetrates a child's life when a parent prays.

What Is Prayer and How Does it Work?

Prayer is much more than just giving a list of desires to God, as if He were the great Sugar Daddy/Santa Claus in the sky. Prayer is acknowledging and experiencing the presence of God and inviting His presence into our lives and circumstances. It's seeking the *presence* of God and releasing the *power* of God which gives us the means to overcome any problem.

The Bible says, "Whatever you bind on earth will be bound in heaven, and whatever you loose on earth will be loosed in heaven" (Matthew 18:18). God gives us authority on earth. When we take that authority, God releases power to us from heaven. Because it's *God's* power and *not* ours, we become the vessel through which His power flows. When we pray, we bring that power to bear upon everything we are praying about, and we allow the power of God to work through our powerlessness. When we pray, we are humbling ourselves before God and saying, "I need Your presence and Your power, Lord. I can't do this without You." When we don't pray, it's like saying we have no need of anything outside of ourselves.

Praying in the name of Jesus is a major key to God's power. Jesus said, "Most assuredly, I say to you, whatever you ask the Father in My name He will give you" (John 16:23). Praying in the name of Jesus gives us authority over the enemy and proves we have faith in God to do what His Word promises. God knows our thoughts and our needs, but He responds to our prayers. That's because He always gives us a choice about everything, including whether we will trust Him and obey by praying in Jesus' name.

Praying not only affects *us,* it also reaches out and touches those for whom we pray. When we pray for our children, we are asking God to make His presence a part of their lives and work powerfully in their behalf. That doesn't mean there will always be an *immediate* response. Sometimes it can take days, weeks, months, or even years. But our prayers are never lost or meaningless. If we are praying, something is happening, whether we can see it or not. The Bible says, "The effective, fervent prayer of a righteous man avails much" (James 5:16). All that needs to happen in our lives and the lives of our children cannot happen without the presence and power of God. Prayer invites and ignites both.

Begin with a Personalized List

I actually started praying for each of my children from the time they were conceived because the Bible says, "He has blessed your children within you" (Psalm 147:13). I believed in the power of prayer. What I *didn't* realize at that time was how important each detail of our lives is to Him. It's not enough to pray only for the concerns of the moment; we need to pray for the future, and we need to pray against the effects of past events. When King David was depressed over what had happened in his life and fearful about future consequences (Psalm 143), he didn't just say, "Oh, well, whatever will be will be." He cried out to God about the past, present, and future of his life. He prayed about *everything*. And that is exactly what we must do as well.

To do this effectively, I found I had to make an extensive personalized list for each child. This wasn't some legalistic obsession that said, "If I don't pray for each specific detail, God won't cover it." I was simply more at peace when I knew God had heard each of my many concerns. So once a year, when we went to the beach for our family vacation, I used those cherished early morning hours before anyone else was up to spend time with God making a master prayer list. I would sit and gaze out over the ocean, pencil and paper in hand, and ask God to show me how to pray for each child over the next twelve months. After all, He was the only one who truly knew what each child needed and what challenges they would face in the future. The Bible says, "The secret of the Lord is with those who fear Him" (Psalm 25:14). He reveals things to us when we ask. God always met me there with good instructions, and I came home with prayer lists for each of my children. Then, throughout the year, I added to them whenever I needed to do so.

I kept many of those lists, and as I look back at them now and see all the answers to my prayers, I'm overcome with the faithfulness of God to work in the lives of our children when we pray.

God's Word as Your Weapon

The battle for our children's lives is waged on our knees. When we don't pray, it's like sitting on the sidelines watching our children in a war zone getting shot at from every angle. When we *do* pray, we're in the battle alongside them, appropriating God's power on their behalf. If we also declare the Word of God in our prayers, then we wield a powerful weapon against which no enemy can prevail.

God's Word is "living and powerful, and sharper than any two-edged sword" (Hebrews 4:12) and it pierces everything it touches. God says His Word, "shall not return to Me void, but it shall accomplish what I please, and it shall prosper in the thing for which I sent it" (Isaiah 55:11). In other words, His Word is *never* ineffectual or without fruit. That's why I've included a number of Bible verses following each of the prayer examples. When you are praying for your child, include an appropriate Scripture verse in your prayer. If you can't think of a verse at the moment you're praying, don't let that stop you, but quote a verse or two whenever you can and you'll see mighty things happen.

As you read the Word during your own devotional time and as you pray for your children with the Holy Spirit's leading, you'll find many more Scriptures to include. And you don't have to have a different verse for each prayer. You may have one or two verses that you use repeatedly during a specific season of intercession for your child. For example, when my daughter went through a period of struggle in school, every time we prayed about it together I encouraged her to quote, "I can do all things through Christ who strengthens me" (Philippians 4:13). When I prayed about the matter by myself, I incorporated the verse, "The righteous cry out, and the LORD hears, and delivers them out of all their troubles" (Psalm 34:17).

When we employ God's Word in prayer, we are laying hold of the promises He gives us and appropriating them into the lives of our children. Through His Word, God guides us, speaks to us, and reminds us He is faithful. In that way, He builds faith in *our* hearts and enables us to understand *His* heart. This helps us to pray boldly in faith, knowing exactly what is *His* truth, *His* will, and *our* authority.

When Jesus spoke to the Devil, He rebuked him. Sometimes in doing this He quoted Scripture. For example, when Satan said to Jesus, "If You will worship before me, all will be Yours," Jesus replied, "Get behind Me, Satan! For it is written, 'You shall worship the Lord your God and Him only you shall serve'" (Luke 4:7–8 NKJV/KJV).

Jesus is our role model. We are to observe Him and do what He does. He said, "Most assuredly I say to you, he who believes in Me, the works that I do he will do also; and greater works than these he will do, because I go to My Father" (John 14:12). He also said, "If you abide in Me, and My words abide in you, you will ask what you desire, and it shall be done for you" (John 15:7). We can resist the Devil more effectively if we pray to God according to His directions found in the Scriptures, and if we understand the power and authority given to us through Jesus Christ. If we . . .

WATCH Him,

WALK with Him,

WAIT on Him,

WORSHIP Him,

and *LIVE* in His word,

WE WILL WIN this battle for our children.

Whenever you pray for your child, do it as if you are interceding for his or her life—because that is *exactly* what you are doing. Remember that while God has a perfect plan for our children's lives, Satan has a plan for them too. Satan's plan is to destroy them, and he will *try* to use any means possible to do so: drugs, sex, alcohol, rebellion, accidents, disease. But he won't be able to successfully use any of those things if his power has been dissipated by prayer. The Bible says, "How can one enter a strong man's house and plunder his goods unless he first binds the strong man?" (Matthew 12:29). In other words, we can't have any effect in the Devil's territory unless we first bind him and forbid him any authority there. Thus, we can also forbid him access to our children's lives.

Of course, Satan can do a lot of damage if we don't teach our children God's ways and God's Word and help them to respect God's laws, and if we don't discipline them, guide them, and help them learn to make godly choices. The Bible tells us, "Train up a child in the way he should go, and when he is old he will not depart from it" (Proverbs 22:6). When we don't do those things, our children can fall into rebellion and make choices that take them out from under the umbrella of God's protection. Prayer and proper instruction in the ways and words of God will make sure that does not happen and that God's plan succeeds—not the Devil's. The Bible says, "Resist the devil and he will flee from you" (James 4:7). Binding Satan's plans in prayer is part of resisting the Devil. Resisting him on behalf of our children can free them to make godly choices.

Satan will always try to make a case against our children so that he can have access into their lives. If we are armed with Scripture, however, he will have to contend with the Word of God. The Bible says, "Now salvation, and strength, and the kingdom of our God, and the power of His Christ have come, for the accuser of our brethren, who accused them before God day and night, has been cast down" (Revelation 12:10). Jesus' death on the cross broke the back of the accuser, but the Evil One will still harass all who don't know their God-given authority over him. This is where our prayers come in. Our children will stand accused until we break the stronghold of the accuser in prayer, using the Word of God as hard evidence against him.

A Good Example of Answered Prayer

From the time our son was about two years old, my husband and I had regular prayer groups in our home. Our church had organized small home groups and we led one of them. Gradually we realized that the needs of our group were too great to handle in one monthly meeting, so we added another night each month just for prayer with the adults. During that time we prayed for every kind of need, but the volume of prayer requests for our children was enormous. As a result, I felt that we needed to have an entire day devoted specifically to praying with and for each of our children. This time of intercession, which we called "Interceding for Our Children's Lives," became so popular that people requested it again and again. In fact, the foundation for this book began over twenty years ago in those very prayer groups. None of us had any idea how important they would become. We only knew we were following the leading of the Lord as we learned how to intercede, and we rejoiced together when we witnessed the many answers to our prayers. (See the Appendix, "Praying Together with Other Parents," for suggestions on how to organize your own time of group intercession for children.)

The Bible says, "If two of you agree on earth concerning anything that they ask, it will be done for them by My father in heaven" (Matthew 18:19). Also, one can put a thousand to flight and two can put ten thousand to flight (Deuteronomy 32:30). It doesn't take much of a mathematical mind to figure out, then, how powerful ten to twelve parents can be when they join in prayer and cry out to God for their children.

In the Scripture I used as the guiding verse for this entire book, God commands, "Pour out your heart like water before the face of the Lord. Lift your hands toward Him for the life of your young children" (Lamentations 2:19). How much clearer can it be that we are to pray with *fervency* and *passion* for our young ones, and look forward to those prayers being answered?

We have had so many answers to the prayers offered during our group times over the last twenty years that I could write a book on those alone, testified to by the parents and children who were involved. However, one specific instance stands out in my mind because it was a direct result of our very *first* prayer time and it was a compelling request for all of us in the group.

Nancy, a single mom, requested prayer for her daughter, Janet, who knew the Lord but was walking away from Him because of her disappointment and hurt over her parents' divorce. One of the specific things we prayed for was Janet's protection, for we knew that children who choose to walk out from under the umbrella of God's blessing open themselves up to all kinds of harm. Within a few weeks of that prayer time, Janet was driving on the freeway late at night and was hit head-on by a drunk driver who had driven up the off-ramp and was traveling full speed in the wrong direction. The doctors said it was a miracle she wasn't killed, but she did have severe injuries to her head, neck, shoulders, and back.

Eventually, through continued prayer and physical therapy, Janet recovered completely, physically and spiritually. She and her mother and all of us who

prayed believe she would not be alive had we not interceded for her life before the accident. Today, Janet is
happily married, with a beautiful daughter of her own,
and she is a devoted Christian woman. She was our
secretary and assistant for eight years, and she will
always be our most wonderful reminder of the power
of a praying parent.

When the Answers Don't Come

Possibly the hardest part of praying for our children is
waiting for our prayers to be answered. Sometimes the
answers come quickly, but many times they do not.
When they don't, we can become discouraged,
despairing, or angry at God. Everything seems hope-
less, and we want to give up. Sometimes, in spite of all
we've done for them and all our prayers for them, our
children make poor choices and then reap the consequences. Those times are hard for a parent to watch,
no matter how old the child.

If your child has made poor choices, don't berate
yourself and stop praying. Keep communication lines
open with your child, continue interceding for him or
her, and declare God's Word. Instead of giving up,
resolve to be even *more* committed to prayer. Pray
with other believers. Stand strong and say, "I've only
begun to fight," keeping in mind that *your* part of the
fight is to pray. *God* actually fights the battle. Remember, too, that your fight is not with your child, it's with

the Devil. *He* is your enemy, not your child. Stand strong in prayer until you see a breakthrough in your child's life.

One of the most encouraging Scriptures I have read with regard to such perseverance is when David said, "I have pursued my enemies and overtaken them; neither did I turn back again till they were destroyed. I have wounded them, so that they were not able to rise; they have fallen under my feet. For You have armed me with strength for the battle" (Psalm 18:37–39). He didn't stop until the job was done and neither should we. We should pray through until we see the answer.

If you have anger or unforgiveness toward God or your child—yes, even loving parents can have these feelings—tell God in total honesty. If you feel disappointment and hopelessness, state it clearly. Don't live with negative emotions and guilt that can separate you from God. Share all of your feelings honestly with Him and then ask Him to forgive you and show you what your next step should be. Above all, don't let any disappointment over unanswered prayer cause you to stop praying.

I Said "Praying," Not "Perfect"

When things go wrong in our children's lives, we blame ourselves. We beat ourselves up for not being perfect parents. But it's not being a perfect parent that makes the difference in a child's life, because there are no perfect parents. None of us are perfect, so how can we be perfect parents? It's being a *praying* parent that makes the difference. And that's something we *all* can be. In fact, we don't even have to be parents. We can be a friend, a teacher, a grandparent, an aunt, a cousin, a neighbor, a guardian, or even a stranger with a heart of compassion or concern for a child. The child may be someone we hear of or read about in the newspaper; the child may even be an adult for whom we have a mother's or father's heart.

If you're aware of a child who doesn't have a praying parent, you can step into the gap right now and answer that need. You can effect a change in the life of any child you care about. All it takes is a heart that says, "God, show me how to pray in a way that will make a difference in this child's life." Then begin with the prayers in this book and see where the Holy Spirit leads you.

At the end of each chapter I have included prayer suggestions for you to use. You may want to pray one each day for a month, or pray one specific prayer for a week, or concentrate on your most pressing concern of the moment until you feel released to move on to another.

Repeat these prayers as often as you like. God didn't say, "Don't come to Me over and over with the same request." In fact, He said to keep on praying, but don't make empty repetitions in your prayers.

And remember, you don't have to keep to any schedule or pray these specific prayers. They are simply a guide to get you going. Begin by submitting yourself to

God and asking Him to help you be the parent and intercessor He wants you to be. Pray as the Holy Spirit leads *you,* as you listen to His prompting in *your* heart for *your* child.

I look forward to hearing about the answers to your prayers.

PRAYER

Lord,

I submit myself to You. I realize that parenting a child in the way You would have me to is beyond my human abilities. I know I need You to help me. I want to partner with You and partake of Your gifts of wisdom, discernment, revelation, and guidance. I also need Your strength and patience, along with a generous portion of Your love flowing through me. Teach me how to love the way You love. Where I need to be healed, delivered, changed, matured, or made whole, I invite You to do that in me. Help me to walk in righteousness and integrity before You. Teach me Your ways, enable me to obey Your commandments and do only what is pleasing in Your sight. May the beauty of Your Spirit be so evident in me that I will be a godly role model. Give me the communication, teaching, and nurturing skills that I must have. Make me the parent You want me to be and teach me how to pray and truly intercede for the life of this child. Lord, You said in Your Word, "Whatever things you ask in prayer, believing, you will receive" (Matthew 21:22). In Jesus' name I ask that You will increase my faith to believe for all the things You've put on my heart to pray for concerning this child.

WEAPONS OF WARFARE

You did not choose Me, but I chose you and appointed you that you should go and bear fruit, and that your fruit should remain, that whatever you ask the Father in My name He may give you.
JOHN 15:16

The righteous man walks in his integrity;
his children are blessed after him.
PROVERBS 20:7

Whatever you ask in My name, that I will do, that the Father may be glorified in the Son. If you ask anything in My name, I will do it.
JOHN 14:13–14

Do not provoke your children to wrath, but bring them up in the training and admonition of the Lord.
EPHESIANS 6:4

Take the helmet of salvation, and the sword
of the Spirit, which is the word of God; praying
always with all prayer and supplication in the Spirit,
being watchful to this end with all perseverance
and supplication for all the saints.
Ephesians **6:17–18**

CHAPTER TWO

Releasing My Child into God's Hands

I didn't have peace when my first child, Christopher, was born because I was concerned about everything. I was afraid that someone might drop him, that he might drown in the bathtub, that he might get deathly ill, that I would forget to feed him, that he would be bitten by a dog, injured in a car accident, kidnapped, or lost. In an act more of desperation than obedience, I cried out to God concerning this. He immediately reminded me that Christopher was a gift to us from Him and that *He* cared even more about our son than we did. I was reminded of the biblical instruction to cast "all your care upon Him" (1 Peter 5:7), and so I did.

"Lord, my son is the biggest 'care' I have, and I release him into Your hands. Only You can raise him right and truly keep him safe. I will no longer strive to do it all by myself but will enter into full partnership with You."

From that point on, whenever I had fear about anything, I immediately took it as a sign to pray until I felt peace. If I didn't have peace right away, then I prayed about it with one or more prayer partners until I did. Daily I released my son to God and asked Him to be in charge of his life. This took the pressure off me and parenting became much more enjoyable.

Over the years I have prayed this kind of prayer many times for each of my children. I prayed it on the first Sunday morning I left them in the church nursery, when they stayed with a baby-sitter overnight, the day they started kindergarten, the times I had to leave them in an operating room so the doctor could stitch them up, their first weekend at a friend's house, the week they flew to Washington D.C. on a field trip, whenever they went away to camp, the morning my son first drove the family car by himself, and every time he played football.

Recently I had to release my son into God's hands again, this time as he left for college. I cried numerous times in the months leading up to that monumental moment of separation, for I realized that our lives would never be the same again. Then, just before the big day, God brought to life the words, "For you shall go out with joy, and be led out with peace; the mountains and the hills shall break forth into singing before you" (Isaiah 55:12). Along with that, He gave me the knowledge and assurance that after the initial pain of releasing our children there comes joy and peace, both for them *and* us. Because we know that no matter what stage of life our children are in, when we release them to God they are in *good hands*. We know that they will go forth in peace and joy and God will make a way for them. He will do the same for us, too. What greater comfort is there? Because of this, on the day we drove to the university to move Christopher into his freshman dorm, I had the joy and peace only God can give, and I was almost certain I heard the mountains and hills singing.

I know I still have many more times ahead when I will have to release my children into God's hands. One of the biggest of all will be when they marry. Whenever I think about this, I am reminded of the Bible story of Hannah, who prayed to God for a son. The Lord answered her prayer and she gave birth to Samuel. Afterward she said, "For this child I prayed, and the Lord has granted me my petition which I asked of Him. Therefore I also have lent him to the Lord; as long as he lives he shall be lent to the Lord" (1 Samuel 1:27–29).

Hannah did such a thorough job of lending him to the Lord that when Samuel was weaned, she took him to the house of the Lord to live with Eli the priest. She did that to fulfill a vow she had made to God concerning Samuel, so don't worry (or get your hopes up, as the case may be); God is not going to ask you to leave your child in the church office for the pastor and his wife to raise. The point is, Hannah released her child to God and then did as He instructed. The result was that Samuel became one of the greatest prophets of God the world has ever known.

We don't want to limit what God can do in our children by clutching them to ourselves and trying to parent them alone. If we're not positive that God is in control of our children's lives, we'll be ruled by fear. And the only way to be sure that God *is* in control is to surrender our hold and allow Him full access to their lives. The way to do that is to live according to His Word and His ways and pray to Him about everything. We can trust God to take care of our children even better than we can. When we release our children into the Father's hands and acknowledge that He is in control of their lives and ours, both we and our children will have greater peace.

We can't be everywhere. But God can. We can't see everything. But God can. We can't know everything. But God can. No matter what age our children are, releasing them into God's hands is a sign of our faith and trust in Him and is the first step toward making a difference in their lives. Prayer for our children begins there.

PRAYER

Lord,

I come to You in Jesus' name and give (name of child) to You. I'm convinced that You alone know what is best for him (her). You alone know what he (she) needs. I release him (her) to You to care for and protect, and I commit myself to pray for everything concerning him (her) that I can think of or that You put upon my heart. Teach me how to pray and guide me in what to pray about.

Help me not to impose my *own* will when I'm praying for him (her), but rather enable me to pray that *Your* will be done in his (her) life.

Thank You that I can partner with You in raising him (her) and that I don't have to do it alone. I'm grateful that I don't have to rely on the world's unreliable and ever-changing methods for child rearing, but that I can have clear directions from Your Word and wisdom as I pray to You for answers.

Thank You, Lord, for the precious gift of this child. Because Your Word says that every good gift comes from You, I know that You have given him (her) to me to care for and raise. Help me to do that. Show me places where I continue to hang on to him (her) and enable me to release him (her) to Your protection, guidance, and counsel. Help me not to live in fear of possible dangers, but in the joy and peace of knowing that You are in control. I rely on You for everything, and this day I trust my child to You and release him (her) into Your hands.

WEAPONS OF WARFARE

If you then, being evil, know how to give good gifts to your children, how much more will your Father who is in heaven give good things to those who ask Him!
MATTHEW 7:11

The mercy of the Lord is from everlasting to
everlasting on those who fear Him, and His
righteousness to children's children. To such as
keep His covenant, and to those who remember
His commandments to do them.
PSALM 103:17–18

They shall not labor in vain, nor bring forth children for
trouble; for they shall be the descendants of the
blessed of the Lord and their offspring with them.
ISAIAH 65:23

Behold, children are a heritage from the Lord,
The fruit of the womb is a reward.
PSALM 127:3

Whatever we ask we receive from Him, because
we keep His commandments and do those things
that are pleasing in His sight.
1 JOHN 3:22

CHAPTER THREE

Securing Protection from Harm

Often our most urgent and fervent prayers regarding our children are for their protection. It's hard to think about other aspects of their lives if we are worried sick over their personal safety. How can we pray about future events when we're concerned about them even having a future?

Living in Los Angeles as we did for the first seventeen years of my son's life and the first twelve years of my daughter's, I had good reason to fear for their safety. Crime rose steadily during those years, and even our "good" neighborhood was no protection against that. So I prayed for God's protection on a daily basis. Actually, I started interceding for my children's safety even *before* they were born, praying for protection from such things as crib death and infant diseases. As they grew, I prayed for protection from violence, molestation, and accidents. I prayed alone, I prayed with my husband, and I prayed with my prayer partners: "Hide (them) under the shadow of Your wings, from the wicked who oppress (them), from (their) deadly enemies who surround them" (Psalm 17:8–9).

Both children suffered their share of minor scrapes, cuts, and common childhood injuries, including a couple that required an emergency room and stitches. However, nothing happened to them that came close to being permanently damaging or serious. That is, until my son was in the car accident which he related to you in the foreword of this book.

Early one morning, shortly after getting fifteen-year-old Christopher and ten-year-old Amanda into their respective carpools and off to school, I received the call that every parent fears.

"Mrs. Omartian, your son is okay, but he's been in a serious car accident and is in the emergency room. It was nearly a head-on collision and none of the three boys in the car were wearing seat belts."

On the way to the hospital, my husband and I prayed for the three boys. As we did, I remembered the times we had laid our hands on Christopher and prayed for him to be protected from car accidents. I remembered the Scripture we had often quoted over him: "For He shall give His angels charge over you, to keep you in all your ways. In their hands they shall bear you up, lest you dash your foot against a stone" (Psalm 91:11–12). God answers prayer and His promises are true. I knew that. If Christopher was in a car accident, God and His angels must have been there protecting him. Then, as I also remembered what the Bible says about the righteous person who fears God—"He will not be afraid of evil tidings; his heart is steadfast, trusting in the Lord" (Psalm 112:7)—I began to feel the peace of God which passes all understanding.

When we arrived at the hospital, we learned that Christopher had been sitting in the backseat of the car with a large duffle bag full of football uniforms on his lap. This cushioned his impact with the back of the front seat and, as a result, he sustained only a bruised knee and a sore back. The boy in the front passenger seat had been thrown through the windshield and was seriously injured. The driver hit the steering wheel and had facial lacerations. The car was totally destroyed.

We and the parents of the other boys could not believe that after all the serious talks we'd had with our sons on the importance of wearing seat belts, they were still not wearing them. Had they obeyed the rules, they might not have been hurt at all. But the good news was that if we had not been praying, they might have been killed or sustained serious and permanent injuries. We *all* knew our sons had been spared because of our prayers in Jesus' name on their behalf, and we were grateful to God.

Being a praying parent doesn't mean that nothing bad will ever happen to your children or that they will never experience pain. They *will,* because pain is a part of life in this fallen world. But the Bible assures us that our prayers play a vital part in keeping trouble from them. And when a painful thing does happen, they will be protected in the midst of it so it will be to their betterment and not their destruction.

This is where the Word of God again plays a vital part in your prayers and your peace. I can't even estimate the number of times I prayed for protection for my family and myself while living in Los Angeles. Every time I asked God to protect us from the random violence that seemed to be everywhere, I quoted these Scriptures: "He delivers me from my enemies. You also lift me up above those who rise against me; You have delivered me from the violent man" (Psalm 18:48). "Blessed be the Lord for He has shown me His marvelous kindness in a strong city!" (Psalm 31:21).

Earthquakes were another major concern in California. I prayed about them all the time, but especially at night before I went to bed. Every bad earthquake I have ever experienced jolted me out of a sound sleep. When that happens you awaken suddenly in pitch blackness with everything around you shaking and a loud noise more frightening than thunder at its mightiest roaring in your ears. That only has to happen once to be implanted in your memory forever. I never went to bed without thinking about earthquakes and praying over our entire family, and I always quoted: "God is our refuge and strength, a very present help in trouble. Therefore we will not fear, even though the earth be removed, and though the mountains be carried into the midst of the sea; though its waters roar and be troubled, though the mountains shake with its swelling" (Psalm 46:1–3).

Even though that Scripture promises safety in the *midst* of the problem, I actually asked for more than that: "Lord, I pray that there would *not* be an earthquake. But if there is one, I pray that we will not be here. Even so, Lord, if it's Your will for us to be here, I pray that You will protect us in it."

I believe God answered that prayer when we moved from Northridge before the earthquake hit that area on January 17, 1994. A few months afterward when my children and I walked through the ruins, we were horrified over how much damage had been done. The house that had been our home was destroyed. But we were most in awe of how God had rescued us and that His hand was on us in response to prayer.

If we had been in the earthquake, I trust that God would have protected us in it, just as He miraculously did for so many others. Disasters can occur anywhere. The point is to pray and trust God to answer.

Things happen when we pray that will not happen when we don't. What might happen, or might *not* happen, to our children if we don't pray today? Let's not wait to find out. Let's get on our knees now.

PRAYER

Lord,

I lift (name of child) up to You and ask that You would put a hedge of protection around her (him). Protect her (his) spirit, body, mind, and emotions from any kind of evil or harm. I pray specifically for protection from accidents, disease, injury, or any other physical, mental, or emotional abuse. I pray that she (he) will make her (his) refuge "in the shadow of Your wings" until "these calamities have passed by" (Psalm 57:1). Hide her (him) from any kind of evil influences that would come against her (him). Keep her (him) safe from any hidden dangers and let no weapon formed against her (him) be able to prosper. Thank You, Lord, for Your many promises of protection. Help her (him) to walk in Your ways and in obedience to Your will so that she (he) never comes out from under the umbrella of that protection. Keep her (him) safe in all she (he) does and wherever she (he) goes. In Jesus' name, I pray.

WEAPONS OF WARFARE

He who dwells in the secret place of the Most High shall abide under the shadow of the Almighty. I will say of the Lord, "He is my refuge and my fortress; my God, in Him I will trust.
PSALM 91:1–2

When you pass through the waters, I will be with you; and through the rivers, they shall not overflow you. When you walk through the fire, you shall not be burned, nor shall the flame scorch you.
ISAIAH 43:2

No weapon formed against you shall prosper, and every
tongue which rises against you in judgment you shall
condemn. This is the heritage of the servants of the
Lord, and their righteousness is from Me, says the LORD.
ISAIAH 54:17

Because you have made the Lord, who is my refuge,
even the Most High, your dwelling place, no evil shall
befall you, nor shall any plague come near your
dwelling.
PSALM 91:9–10

I will both lie down in peace, and sleep; for You alone,
O LORD, make me dwell in safety.
PSALM 4:8

CHAPTER FOUR

Feeling Loved and Accepted

One of the difficult things children must deal with are the lies that can come into their minds masquerading as truth: "I'm not loved," "I'm not accepted," "I'm not appreciated," "I'm not attractive," "I'm not good enough," "I'm too fat," "too thin," "too tall," "too short," "too dumb," "too smart," "too everything." These lies escalate as children move into their teenage years and often are carried into adulthood. That's why I'm convinced it's never too soon to start praying for a child to feel loved and accepted—first by God, then by family, then by peers and others. We can start when they are babies, or whatever age your child *is* at this moment, and pray about this concern throughout their lives.

The opposite of being loved and accepted is being rejected—something we've all experienced at one time or another in our lives. Who among us has never felt embarrassment, humiliation, failure, fault, or someone's disapproval over something we've done? Whether it be by a family member, a friend, or a complete stranger, rejection happens to all of us. Some people can let such incidents roll off their backs, because they know, deep within, that they are accepted. Others, however, may bear deep emotional wounds from incident after incident of rejection, so any perceived lack of acceptance can transform their personalities into something ugly. That's why rejection is at the root of so much of the evil we read about in the newspapers every day. A rejected worker goes back to his former place of employment and shoots his boss and co-workers. A rejected husband beats or kills his wife. A mother who has been rejected by others abuses her child. Rejection brings out the worst in people. Love and acceptance bring out the best. A person who already feels rejected interprets everything as rejection—a mere look, a harmless word, an insignificant action—while someone who feels loved and accepted thinks nothing of the same look, word, or action. A person may *not* actually be rejected, but if he (she) *believes* he (she) is, the effect is just as damaging as if it were true.

The love of God, however, can change all this. Knowing that God loves and accepts us changes our lives. He says, "I have chosen you and not cast you away" (Isaiah 41:9). "I have loved you with an everlasting love" (Jeremiah 31:3). And He proves His love because "God demonstrates His own love toward us, in that while we were still sinners, Christ died for us" (Romans 5:8). On top of that, the Bible assures us that "neither death nor life, nor angels nor principalities nor powers, nor things present nor things to come, nor height nor depth, nor any other created thing, shall be able to separate us from the love of God which is in Christ Jesus our Lord (Romans 8:38–39).

We must pray that our children understand these truths; they are the solid ground upon which love and acceptance are established in their character.

Even though it is God's love that is ultimately most important in anyone's life, a parent's love (or lack thereof) is perceived and felt first. Parental love is the first love a child experiences and the first love he (she) understands. In fact, parental love is often the means by which children actually open themselves to God's love and come to understand it early in life. That's why from the time our children are born, we should pray, "God help me to really love my child the way You want me to and teach me how to show it in a way he (she) can understand." If, however, your child is now older and you realize for one reason or another that he (she) doesn't feel loved, you can begin right now asking God to penetrate his (her) heart with *His* love and open it to receive *your* love and the love of others.

Ask God to show you what you can do to communicate love to your child—and don't listen to the Devil weighing *you* down with guilt about past failure. You know his tactics:

"Your child doesn't feel loved because you're a terrible parent."

"If you weren't so dysfunctional you'd be able to communicate love to your child."

"No one ever loved you, so how can you love anyone else?"

These are lies from the pit of Hell and part of Satan's plan for your child's life.

If you are being tormented by guilt or feelings of failure in this area, confess your thoughts to God, pray about it, put it in God's hands, and then stand up and proclaim the truth. Say, "God loves my child. I love my child. Other people love my child. If my child doesn't feel loved it's because he (she) has believed the lies of the enemy. We refuse to live according to Satan's lies." Although you may have to persist for a while on this, don't give up resisting the Devil's lies by speaking God's truth. Then pray for God's love to penetrate your child's heart, as well as for your love to be perceived and received.

Along with prayer, children need to see love manifested toward them with eye contact, physical touch (a pat, a hug, a kiss), and with loving acts, deeds, and words. I found that when I made a deliberate effort to look my children directly in the eye with my hands gently touching them and with a smile say, "I love you and I think you're great," I could *always* see an immediate and noticeable change in their face and demeanor. Try it and you'll see what I mean. It may feel awkward at first if you've never done it before, or if your child is older or even an adult, but go ahead and do it anyway. If you are hesitant, pray that God will enable you to do it and that it will be well received.

If you feel you don't have the love you need to give your child, ask the Holy Spirit for it. The Bible says,

"The love of God has been poured out in our hearts by the Holy Spirit who was given to us" (Romans 5:5). One of God's main purposes for your life is to fill you with so much of His love that it overflows onto others. Praying for your child will not only be a sign of that love in your heart, it could also be the very means by which that love is multiplied to overflowing.

PRAYER

Lord,

I pray for (name of child) to feel loved and accepted. Penetrate his (her) heart with Your love right now and help him (her) to fully understand how far-reaching and complete it is. Your Word says You loved us so much that You sent Your Son to die for us (John 3:16). Deliver him (her) from any lies of the Enemy that may have been planted in his (her) mind to cause him (her) to doubt that. Jesus said, "As the Father loved Me, I also have loved you; abide in My love" (John 15:9–10). Lord, help (name of child) to abide in Your love. May he (she) say as David did, "Cause me to hear Your lovingkindness in the morning, for in You do I trust" (Psalm 143:8). Manifest Your love to this child in a real way today and help him (her) to receive it.

I pray also that You would help me to love this child unconditionally the way You do, and enable me to show it in a manner he (she) can perceive.

Reveal to me how I can demonstrate and model Your love to him (her) so that it will be clearly understood. I pray that all my family members will love and accept him (her), and may he (she) find favor with other people as well. With each day that he (she) grows in the confidence of being loved and accepted, release in him (her) the capacity to easily *communicate* love to others. Enable him (her) to reach out in love in a way that is appropriate. As he (she) comes to fully understand the depth of Your love for him (her) and receives it into his (her) soul, make him (her) a vessel through which Your love flows to others. In Jesus' name I pray.

WEAPONS OF WARFARE

In this the love of God was manifested toward us, that God has sent His only begotten Son into the world, that we might live through Him. In this is love, not that we loved God, but that He loved us and sent His Son to be the propitiation for our sins. Beloved, if God so loved us, we also ought to love one another.

1 John 4:9–11

For you are a holy people to the Lord your God; the Lord your God has chosen you to be a people for Himself, a special treasure above all the peoples on the face of the earth.

Deuteronomy 7:6

We have known and believed the love that God
has for us. God is love, and he who abides in
love abides in God, and God in him.
1 JOHN 4:16

We are bound to give thanks to God always for you,
brethren beloved by the Lord, because God from the
beginning chose you for salvation through sanctification by the Spirit and belief in the truth.
2 THESSALONIANS 2:13

Blessed be the God and Father of our Lord Jesus
Christ, who has blessed us with every spiritual blessing
in the heavenly places in Christ, just as He chose us in
Him before the foundation of the world, that we should
be holy and without blame before Him in love, having
predestined us to adoption as sons by Jesus Christ to
Himself, according to the good pleasure of His will,
to the praise of the glory of His grace, by which He
has made us accepted in the Beloved.
EPHESIANS 1:3–6

CHAPTER FIVE

Establishing an Eternal Future

Above all else, we want our children to come to a knowledge of who God really is and to know Jesus as their Savior. When that happens, we know their eternal future is secure; we know that when they die, we will see them again in heaven. What a wonderful hope that is!

Debby Boone and her husband, Gabri, who participated in some of the "Interceding for Your Child's Life" prayer groups, asked me to write a song for one of Debby's albums that she could sing as an anthem of the heart to her children. I wrote the following lyrics to a song called "Above All Else," which my husband put to music and Debby recorded and now sings in her concerts. These words, I believe, sum up what is in every believing parent's heart.

> *So much to say and just a lifetime left to say it.*
> *How quickly time passes.*
> *If I had my way, I'd keep you safe within my arms*
> *While the storm of life crashes.*

I won't always be with you, my child, but words I
     can give.
When the winds of hope are dying down, these
     words will live.
Above all else, know God's the One who'll never
     leave you.
Look to Him above all else.
He is love you can depend upon, a heart set to care.
If in the darkest night you should be lost, He will be
     there.
He's the Everlasting Father,
In His hands you'll never fall.
He's the One who holds it all,
Above all else.
He's the Author of your laughter,
He's the Keeper of your tears,
He's the One who you must fear
Above all else.
He's the Giver of the kingdom
Bought for you right from the start,
And He'll ask you for your heart
Above all else.

So much to say
And not enough time left to say it.
Just love the Lord
Above all else.

Copyright 1987 by Michael and Stormie Omartian for See This House Music /
ASCAP

My son and daughter both made a decision to receive Jesus into their lives when they were around five years of age. We had taught them about the things of God, read Bible stories to them, prayed with them daily, and took them regularly to church, where they were instructed in God's ways. They had much exposure to the idea of receiving Jesus, but we never forced it on them or asked them to make a decision. Instead, we prayed that what they learned would penetrate their heart and give them a desire for a close relationship with God. We wanted that decision to come from their heart and be theirs alone. When that moment occurred, each child started a conversation with us by asking questions about Jesus and ended up wanting us to pray with them to receive Him as Savior. My husband and I have great peace knowing our son's and daughter's eternal future is joy-filled and secure.

No matter what age your children are, it's never too early or too late to start praying for their salvation. Jesus said, "Most assuredly, I say to you, unless one is born again, he cannot see the kingdom of God" (John 3:3). He also said, "Behold, I stand at the door and knock. If anyone hears My voice and opens the door, I will come in to him and dine with him, and he with Me" (Revelation 3:20). We want our children to open the door of their hearts to Jesus and experience God's kingdom, both in this life and forever after. Remember, if *you* don't pray for your children's eternal future, they may not have the kind you want them to have.

Once our children have received the Lord, we must continue praying for their relationship with Him. How many times have we heard of children who walk with God when they're young, but turn away from Him in their teens or adulthood? We want our children to always be "filled with the knowledge of His will in all wisdom and spiritual understanding" and to "walk worthy of the Lord, fully pleasing Him, being fruitful in every good work and increasing in the knowledge of God" (Colossians 1:9–10). Paul and Timothy prayed this for the children of God in Colosse, and we should pray it for our children. There is always more and more of the life of the Lord for each of us to open up to and experience. Praying for the Lord to pour out His Spirit upon our children must be our ongoing prayer.

PRAYER

Lord,

I bring (name of child) before You and ask that You would help her (him) grow into a deep understanding of who You are. Open her (his) heart and bring her (him) to a full knowledge of the truth about You. Lord, You have said in Your Word, "If you confess with your mouth the Lord Jesus and believe in your heart that God has raised Him from the dead, you will be saved" (Romans 10:9). I pray for that kind of faith for my child. May she (he) call You her (his) Savior, be filled with Your Holy Spirit, acknowledge You in every area of her (his) life, and choose always to follow You and Your ways. Help her (him) to fully believe that Jesus laid down His life for her (him) so that she (he) might have life eternally and abundantly now. Help her (him) to comprehend the fullness of Your forgiveness so that she (he) will not live in guilt and condemnation.

I pray that she (he) will live a fruitful life, ever increasing in the knowledge of You. May she (he) always know Your will, have spiritual understanding, and walk in a manner that is pleasing in Your sight. You have said in Your Word that You will pour out Your Spirit on my offspring (Isaiah 44:3). I pray that You would pour out Your Spirit upon (name of child) this day.

Thank You, Lord, that You care about her (his) eternal future even more than I do and that it is secure in You. In Jesus' name I pray that she (he) will not doubt or stray from the path You have for her (him) all the days of her (his) life.

WEAPONS OF WARFARE

This is the will of Him who sent Me, that
everyone who sees the Son and believes
in Him may have everlasting life; and I
will raise him up at the last day.
JOHN 6:40

For this is good and acceptable in the sight of God our
Savior, who desires all men to be saved and to come
to the knowledge of the truth.
1 TIMOTHY 2:3–4

We know that the Son of God has come and has given
us an understanding, that we may know Him who is
true; and we are in Him who is true, in His Son Jesus
Christ. This is the true God and eternal life.
1 JOHN 5:20

This is the testimony: that God has given us eternal
life, and this life is in His Son.
1 JOHN 5:11

And I will pray to the Father, and He will give
you another Helper, that He may abide with you
forever—the Spirit of truth, whom the world
cannot receive, because it neither sees Him nor
knows Him; but you know Him, for He
dwells with you and will be in you.
JOHN 14:16–17

CHAPTER SIX

Honoring Parents and Resisting Rebellion

It seems odd to *require* someone to honor us, doesn't it? If it's really honor, shouldn't they do it without being told? Well, this may be true concerning other people in our lives, but not our children. They must be taught.

The Bible says, "Children, obey your parents in the Lord, for this is right. Honor your father and mother, which is the first commandment with promise: that it may be well with you and you may live long on the earth" (Ephesians 6:1–3). If our children disobey this command of the Lord, they could not only be cut off from all God has for them, but their lives could be cut short as well. The Bible also says, "Whoever curses his father or his mother, his lamp will be put out in deep darkness" (Proverbs 20:20). The fact that we can affect the length and quality of our children's lives is reason enough to pray, instruct, and discipline them. Along with that, we must recognize and resist any rebellion that threatens to creep into their minds and cause them to do other than God commands.

Rebellion is actually pride put into action. Rebellious thoughts say, "I'm going to do what I want, no matter what God or anyone else says about it." The Bible says "rebellion is as the sin of witchcraft" (1 Samuel 15:23) because its ultimate end is total opposition to God. That same verse also says that "stubbornness is as iniquity and idolatry." Pride gets us into rebellion, but stubbornness is what *keeps* us there. Anyone who walks in rebellion has a stubborn idol in his or her life. When children do not honor their father or mother, it is often the first sign that the idols in a child's heart—a child of any age—are pride and selfishness. That's why children who are not taught to obey their parents become rebellious. They say, "I want what I want when I want it."

"Woe to the rebellious children," says the Lord, "Who take counsel, but not of Me, and who devise plans, but not of My Spirit, that they may add sin to sin" (Isaiah 30:1). Identifying and destroying the idols of pride and selfishness through prayer can often be the key to breaking a child's rebellion.

The opposite of rebellion is obedience, or walking in the will of God. Obedience brings great security and the confidence of knowing you're where you're supposed to be, doing what you're supposed to do. The Bible promises that if we are obedient we will be blessed, but if we are not we will dwell in darkness and be destroyed. We don't want that for our children. We want our children to walk in obedience so that they will have confidence, security, long life, and peace. One of the first steps of obedience for children is to obey and honor their parents. This is something a child must be taught, but teaching becomes easier when prayer paves the way.

When my son was fourteen years old, he covered his bedroom walls with posters of the musicians he admired most. The problem was that in some of the pictures both the attire and the music being represented were offensive to his father and me and not glorifying to God. When we asked Christopher to take those particular posters down and explained why, he balked, then with a less than humble spirit did what we asked. A short time later, however, he replaced them with new ones which were just as bad. We again confronted him, took appropriate disciplinary measures, and this time *we* took them *all* down for him.

Christopher was not happy, and we recognized we were dealing with the early manifestations of a rebellious spirit. So we decided to do as the Bible says and "Put on the whole armor of God that you may be able to stand against the wiles of the devil" (Ephesians 6:11). We prayed, we employed the Word of God, and we professed our faith in God's ability to make us overcomers. We did battle in the Spirit and witnessed the peace of God take control of the situation. Our son's attitude changed, and the next time he put up posters they met the requirements we, as his parents, had established. This was the power of God in action, employed by praying parents.

Wall posters seem like such a minor issue now, but at the time we were dealing with a strong will that was exalting itself over parents and God. And by resisting that display of rebellion, we were able to stop it before it became something major. We were determined to win the struggle because we knew we had God and His Word on our side and because, for our son, something eternal was at stake.

If your child is older, an adolescent or even an adult, and rebellion is already clearly manifested in his or her behavior, the discipline and teaching part will be harder, but you still have the power of prayer. Remember, your battle is not with your son or daughter. "For we do not wrestle against flesh and blood, but against principalities, against powers, against the rulers of the darkness of this age, against spiritual hosts of wickedness in the heavenly places" (Ephesians 6:12). Your battle is with the Enemy. The good news is that Jesus has given you authority "over all the power of the enemy" (Luke 10:19). Don't be afraid to take advantage of that.

Rebellion will surface in your child at one time or another. Be ready to meet the challenge with prayer and the Word of God, along with correction, discipline, and teaching. Don't be intimidated by a rebellious spirit. Jesus is Lord above that, too.

PRAYER

Lord,
   I pray that You would give (name of child) a heart that desires to obey You. Put into him (her) a longing to spend time with You, in Your Word and in prayer, listening for Your voice. Shine Your light upon any secret or unseen rebellion that is taking root in his (her) heart, so that it can be identified

and destroyed. Lord, I pray that he (she) will not give himself (herself) over to pride, selfishness, and rebellion, but that he (she) will be delivered from it. By the authority You've given me in Jesus' name, I "stand against the wiles of the devil" and I resist idolatry, rebellion, stubbornness, and disrespect; they will have no part in my son's (daughter's) life, nor will my child walk a path of destruction and death because of them.

Your Word instructs, "Children, obey your parents in all things, for this is well pleasing to the Lord" (Colossians 3:20). I pray that You would turn the heart of this child toward his (her) parents and enable him (her) to honor and obey father and mother so that his (her) life will be long and good. Turn his (her) heart toward You so that all he (she) does is pleasing in Your sight. May he (she) learn to identify and confront pride and rebellion in himself (herself) and be willing to confess and repent of it. Make him (her) uncomfortable with sin. Help him (her) to know the beauty and simplicity of walking with a sweet and humble spirit in obedience and submission to You.

WEAPONS OF WARFARE

If you are willing and obedient, you shall eat the good of the land; but if you refuse and rebel, you shall be devoured by the sword; for the mouth of the Lord has spoken.

ISAIAH 1:19–20

Those who sat in darkness and in the shadow of death,
bound in affliction and irons—because they rebelled
against the words of God, and despised the counsel of
the Most High, therefore He brought
down their heart with labor; they fell down,
and there was none to help.
PSALM 107:10–12

The eye that mocks his father, and scorns obedience
to his mother, the ravens of the valley will pick
it out, and the young eagles will eat it.
PROVERBS 30:17

My son, hear the instruction of your father, and do
not forsake the law of your mother; for they will
be graceful ornaments on your head, and
chains about your neck.
PROVERBS 1:8–9

Nevertheless they were disobedient and rebelled
against You. . . . Therefore You delivered them
into the hand of their enemies who
oppressed them.
NEHEMIAH 9:26–27

CHAPTER SEVEN

Maintaining Good Family Relationships

My sister and I experienced a major breach in our relationship a number of years ago and ended up not communicating with each other for two years. All this was due to a complete misunderstanding. Our own individual hurts had masked our ability to see clearly what was happening in each other's personality and lives. We were in two different worlds, even though we had been raised in the same house within the same family. This whole episode was very upsetting to me, and I didn't stop praying about it until my sister and I were finally reconciled and our relationship restored. However, I believe if we'd had praying parents, it wouldn't have happened in the first place.

One of the things the Enemy of our soul likes to do is get into the middle of God-ordained relationships and cause them to misfire, miscommunicate, short-circuit, fracture, or disconnect. The more a family can be splintered apart, the weaker and more ineffectual they become and the more the Enemy has control of their lives. The way to avoid this is through prayer. When you cover your family relationships in prayer, whether it be with children, parents, stepparents, brothers, sisters, grandparents, aunts, uncles, cousins, husband, or wife, there will be far fewer instances of strained or severed relationships.

When my daughter was born, her brother was four and a half years old. I prayed from the beginning that Christopher and Amanda would have a close relationship with each other, and I did all I could to see that happen. Their friendship was so tight in their early years that other people noticed and remarked about it. Then one day Christopher became a teenager and everything changed. He suddenly had places to go and people to see and no longer had time for his little sister. The humorous put downs he enjoyed with his friends were not well received by his younger female sibling. Feeling rejected and hurt, she would retaliate. I became a referee and it grieved my heart to see what was happening.

Then one day I realized something important: because everything had been going so well between Amanda and Christopher, I had stopped praying about their relationship. So I began praying about it again, wishing I had never stopped. It took some time, but little by little I observed a softening in their attitude toward one another. I know that if I had done nothing there would most likely have been the same permanent breach between them as there have been in too many relationships in my family's past. Although my children's relationship is still not where I want it to be, it's getting stronger all the time. And I will continue to hold up this matter in prayer as long as I'm alive.

How many family relationships are left to chance because no one prays about them? Far too many, I suspect. It's sad to see families split apart and individual members have nothing to do with one another when they are grown. It's heartbreaking to think of that happening with our own children. Yet it doesn't have to be that way.

In Isaiah 58, God tells of all the wonderful things that will happen when we fast and pray. He says, "You shall raise up the foundations of many generations; and you shall be called the Repairer of the Breach" (Isaiah 58:12). God wants us to restore unity, to maintain the family bonds in the Lord, and to leave a spiritual inheritance of solidarity that can last for generations.

The Bible also says, "Be of the same mind toward one another. Do not set your mind on high things, but associate with the humble. Do not be wise in your own opinion" (Romans 12:16). We need to pray for humility and unity.

Jesus said, "Blessed are the peacemakers, for they shall be called the sons of God" (Matthew 5:9). I say, let's be peacemakers. There are obviously not enough of us in the world. "Let us pursue the things which make for peace and the things by which one may edify another" (Romans 14:19). Let's begin by praying for those closest to us—our children—and branch out from there.

PRAYER

Lord,

    I pray for (name of child) and her (his) relationship with all family members. Protect and preserve them from any unresolved or permanent breach. Fill her (his) heart with Your love and give her (him) an abundance of compassion and forgiveness that will overflow to each member of the family. Specifically, I pray for a close, happy, loving, and fulfilling relationship between (name of child) and (name of family member) for all the days of their lives. May there always be good communication between them and may unforgiveness have no root in their hearts. Help them to love, value, appreciate, and respect one another so that the God-ordained tie between them cannot be broken. I pray according to Your Word, that they "be kindly affectionate to one another with brotherly love, in honor giving preference to one another" (Romans 12:10).

    Teach my child to resolve misunderstandings according to Your Word. And if any division has already begun, if any relationship is strained or severed, Lord, I pray that You will drive out the wedge of division and bring healing. I pray that there be no strain, breach, misunderstanding, arguing, fighting, or separating of ties. Give her (him) a heart of forgiveness and reconciliation.

Your Word instructs us to "be of one mind, having compassion for one another; love as brothers, be tenderhearted, be courteous" (1 Peter 3:8). Help her (him) to live accordingly, "endeavoring to keep the unity of the Spirit in the bond of peace" (Ephesians 4:3). In Jesus' name I pray that You would instill a love and compassion in her (him) for all family members that is strong and unending, like a cord that cannot be broken.

WEAPONS OF WARFARE

Blessed are the peacemakers, for they shall
be called sons of God.
MATTHEW 5:9

Behold, how good and how pleasant it is for
brethren to dwell together in unity!
PSALM 133:1

Now may the God of patience and comfort grant you to
be like-minded toward one another, according to Christ
Jesus, that you may with one mind and one mouth glorify the God and Father of our Lord Jesus Christ.
ROMANS 15:5–6

If it is possible, as much as depends on you, live
peaceably with all men.
ROMANS 12:18

Now I plead with you, brethren, by the name of our
Lord Jesus Christ, that you all speak the same thing,
and that there be no divisions among you, but that
you be perfectly joined together in the same mind
and in the same judgment.

1 CORINTHIANS 1:10

CHAPTER EIGHT

Attracting Godly Friends and Role Models

I have always prayed for my children's friends and, for the most part, they've had great ones. Occasionally they've made friends that, as a parent, I had reservations about. Not because I didn't like them; actually, in every instance, I liked them very much. What I didn't like was the type of influence they were on my child, and what the combination of that child and mine produced. The way I always handled this situation was to pray. I prayed for that child to be changed or else be taken out of my child's life. In every case that prayer was answered. In several instances, the passage of time revealed the accuracy of my apprehension. The children I was concerned about turned out to have trouble-filled lives.

Parents often have gut-level feelings about their children's friends. When that happens, ask God for Holy Spirit-inspired discernment and pray accordingly.

One of my most fervent times of intercession regarding my children's friends came when we moved from California to Tennessee. We made the move just as my son was starting his senior year of high school and my daughter was beginning seventh grade—the two worst times for children to change schools. Normally I wouldn't have wanted my children to change schools at that time, but in this instance my husband and I felt the clear leading of the Lord to make the move. Because I knew how difficult this time could be for my children, every day in the months before and after we moved I prayed, "Lord, help my children to make godly friends. I know that *You* brought us here and You will not leave my children forsaken. I'm concerned that in their need for acceptance they'll end up with friends whose moral standards are not as high as Yours. Bring godly role models into their lives."

The first six months were very lonely times for both Christopher and Amanda, and I often lay awake at night praying on their behalf. There was nothing else I could do. I couldn't intervene and hook them up with good friends as I might have when they were younger. But even if I'd been able to do that, I never would have done as good a job as God did in answer to my prayers. Eventually people came into their lives who have become some of the greatest friends they've ever had. This is not just a coincidence or a fairy tale ending. This is a result of intercessory prayer. This is the result of crying out to God, saying,

"God, help my children to attract godly friends and role models."

God's Word clearly instructs us: "Do not be unequally yoked together with unbelievers. For what fellowship has righteousness with lawlessness? And what communion has light with darkness? And what accord has Christ with Belial? Or what part has a believer with an unbeliever?" (2 Corinthians 6:14–15). That doesn't mean our children can never have a non-believing friend. But there is clear implication that their closest friends, the ones to whom they have strong ties, should be believers. "Can two walk together, unless they are agreed?" (Amos 3:3). No, they can't. That means if they are not agreed, somebody has to change. And that's why "The righteous should choose his friends carefully, for the way of the wicked leads them astray" (Proverbs 12:26).

If your child doesn't have close believing friends, begin to pray right now toward that end. Pray for the unbelieving friends to receive the Lord and for strong believing friends to come into their lives. Too often parents feel helpless to do anything about the bad influence of certain people in their children's lives. But we are not helpless. We have the *power of God* and the *truth of His Word* behind us. Don't stand for someone leading your child astray. There is too much written in Scripture about the importance of the company we keep to take a passive approach to this issue.

One of the greatest influences in our children's lives will be their friends and role models. How can we *not* pray about them?

PRAYER

Lord,
I lift up (name of child) to You and ask that You would bring godly friends and role models into his (her) life. Give him (her) the wisdom he (she) needs to choose friends who are godly and help him (her) to never compromise his (her) walk with You in order to gain acceptance. Give me Holy Spirit-inspired discernment in how I guide or influence him (her) in the selection of friends. I pray that You would take anyone who is *not* a godly influence *out* of his (her) life or else transform that person into Your likeness.

Your Word says, "He who walks with wise men will be wise, but the companion of fools will be destroyed" (Proverbs 13:20). Don't let my child be a companion of fools. Enable him (her) to walk with wise friends and not have to experience the destruction that can happen by walking with foolish people. Deliver him (her) from anyone with an ungodly character so he (she) will not learn that person's ways and set a snare for his (her) own soul.

Whenever there is grief over a lost friendship, comfort him (her) and send new friends with whom he (she) can connect, share, and be the person You created him (her) to be. Take away any loneliness or low self-esteem that would cause him (her) to seek out less than God-glorifying relationships.

In Jesus' name I pray that You would teach him (her) the meaning of true friendship. Teach him (her) how to be a good friend and make strong, close, lasting relationships. May each of his (her) friendships always glorify You.

WEAPONS OF WARFARE

Do not enter the path of the wicked, and do
not walk in the way of evil.
PROVERBS 4:14

I have written to you not to keep company with
anyone named a brother, who is sexually immoral,
or covetous, or an idolater, or a reviler, or a
drunkard, or an extortioner—not even to eat
with such a person.
1 CORINTHIANS 5:11

My son, fear the Lord and the king; do not associate
with those given to change; for their calamity will
rise suddenly, and who knows the ruin those
two can bring?
PROVERBS 24:21–22

Make no friendship with an angry man, and with
a furious man do not go, lest you learn his ways
and set a snare for your soul.
PROVERBS 22:24–25

Blessed is the man who walks not in the counsel of the
ungodly, nor stands in the path of sinners,
nor sits in the seat of the scornful.
PSALM 1:1

CHAPTER NINE

Developing a Hunger for the Things of God

When we read in the newspaper about young people stealing, killing, destroying property, or being sexually promiscuous, we can be sure that those individuals do not have a healthy fear of the Lord, nor a good understanding of His ways, nor a hunger for the things of God. Some of these young people may even be from Christian families and have received Jesus, but because they haven't been taught to fear God and desire His presence they are controlled by their flesh.

Fearing God means having a deeply committed respect, love, and reverence for God's authority and power. It means being afraid of what life would be like without Him and being grateful that because of His love we'll never have to experience such despair. It means hungering for all that God is and all that He has for us.

There is so much in the world to divert our children's attention away from the things of God, and the Devil will come to each child with his agenda and plan to see if they will buy into it. But when we do our part to teach, instruct, discipline, and train our children in the ways of God . . .

when we read them stories from God's Word,

when we teach them how to pray and have faith that God is who He says He is and will do what He says He'll do,

when we help them get plugged in with godly friends,

when we show them that walking with God brings joy and fulfillment, not boredom and restrictions,

when we pray with and for them about everything, . . . then our children will develop a hunger for the things of God.

They will know that the things of God are top priority.

They will become God-controlled and not flesh-controlled.

They will long for His ways, His Word, and His presence.

They will fear God and live a longer and better life.

For "The fear of the Lord prolongs days, but the years of the wicked will be shortened" (Proverbs 10:27).

When my husband and I knew we were moving from California to Tennessee, the first thing we prayed about was finding a great church with an excellent youth group. That prayer was answered, and it was the main reason our children were able to make this major adjustment successfully; for it was in their new church and youth group that they found godly friends and continued growing in their relationship with the Lord. Finding a church that is actively teaching God's Word, showing God's love, and sharing God's joy with its children and young people will make a big difference in helping your children develop a hunger for the things of God.

Start right now by praying for your child to fear God, have faith in Him and His Word, and develop the kind of heart that seeks after Him. This could be the determining factor in whether your child will have a constant struggle living in the flesh or be fulfilled and blessed living in the Spirit. Remember, "there is no want to those who fear Him" (Psalm 34:9). It's never too early to begin praying about this. Don't wait another moment.

PRAYER

Lord,

I pray for (name of child) to have an ever-increasing hunger for more of You. May she (he) long for Your presence—long to spend time with You in prayer, praise, and worship. Give her (him) a desire for the truth of Your Word and a love for Your laws and Your ways. Teach her (him) to live by faith and be led by the Holy Spirit, having an availability to do what You tell her (him) to do. May she (he) be so aware of the fullness of Your Holy Spirit in her (him) that when she (he) is depleted in any way she (he) will immediately run to You to be renewed and refreshed.

I pray that her (his) heart will not have any allegiances or diversions away from You, but rather that she (he) would be repulsed by ungodliness and all that is in opposition to You. May a deep reverence and love for You and Your ways color everything she (he) does and every choice she (he) makes. Help her (him) to understand the consequences of her (his) actions and know that a life controlled by the flesh will only reap death. May she (he) not be wise in her (his) own eyes, but rather "fear the Lord and depart from evil" (Proverbs 3:7).

I pray that she (he) will be reliable, dependable, responsible, compassionate, sensitive, loving, and giving to others. Deliver her (him) from any pride, laziness, slothfulness, selfishness, or lust of the flesh. I pray that she (he) will have a teachable and submissive spirit that says "Yes" to the things of God and "No" to the things of the flesh. Strengthen her (him) to stand strong in her (his) convictions.

I pray that she (he) will always desire to be an active member of a Christian church that is alive to the truth of Your Word and the power of Holy Spirit-led worship, prayer, and teaching. As she (he) learns to read Your Word, write Your law in her (his) mind and on her (his) heart so that she (he) always walks with a confident assurance of the righteousness of Your commands. As she (he) learns to pray, may she (he) also learn to listen for Your voice. I pray that her (his) relationship with You will never become lukewarm, indifferent, or shallow. May there always be a Holy Spirit fire in her (his) heart and an unwavering desire for the things of God.

❧

WEAPONS OF WARFARE

Blessed are those who hunger and thirst for righteousness, for they shall be filled.
MATTHEW 5:6

The fear of the Lord is a fountain of life, to turn one away from the snares of death.
PROVERBS 14:27

I have been crucified with Christ; it is no longer I who live, but Christ lives in me; and the life which I now live in the flesh I live by faith in the Son of God, who loved me and gave Himself for me.
GALATIANS 2:20

Blessed are those who keep His testimonies, who seek Him with the whole heart!
PSALM 119:2

Teach me Your way, O LORD; I will walk in Your truth; unite my heart to fear Your name. I will praise You, O Lord my God, with all my heart, and I will glorify Your name forevermore.
PSALM 86:11–12

CHAPTER TEN

Being the Person God Created

I know a man who gave up his high-paying job as an engineer for a large company in order to become an auto mechanic. He did it because he loved doing auto repair more than anything else. He was not only the best mechanic in town, but also a happy and fulfilled person. I know another man who refused to follow the call of God to be a pastor because he wanted to be a successful businessman instead. He eventually lost his family through divorce, suffered the death of his young son, and saw his life dissipate into sadness and loss. How different it all might have been if he'd had a praying parent or someone helping him to understand who God made him to be.

Not knowing who God made us to be, trying to be who we are *not*, or even just *desiring* to be someone else, can only lead to a life of misery, frustration, and unfulfillment. We see examples of this in adults who work at jobs they hate, living miserable lives that always fall short of their expectations. You can be sure that at some point such persons bought into a lie that says, "Who I am is not good enough. I need to be someone else." Perhaps they've never been encouraged to recognize their God-given strengths and talents. Certainly they've not realized who God made them to be.

We become the person God created us to be when we ask God for guidance and then do what He tells us to do. The prophet Jeremiah kept telling the people of Israel what God wanted them to hear, but they refused to listen. Finally, the Lord said, "Behold, I will bring on Judah and on all the inhabitants of Jerusalem all the doom that I have pronounced against them; because I have spoken to them but they have not heard, and I have called to them but they have not answered" (Jeremiah 35:17). Destructive things happen to us when we don't respond to God's voice. We can pray that our children have ears to hear God's voice so such misery doesn't happen to them.

One of the Devil's plans for young people is to get them to compare themselves with others, judge themselves as deficient, and then seek to be someone they were not created to be. Young girls compare themselves to other girls and see them as having prettier hair, nicer clothes, a better house, greater popularity, higher scholastic achievement, or more talent and beauty. Young boys look at other boys and see them as taller, better looking, greater athletes, having more friends, more hair, more possessions, or more skills and ability. This day after day comparing and falling short can attack the true identity of a child. I've known far too many young people who, by the time they reach their teens, long to be someone other than who they are. Instead of appreciating who God made them to be and spending their energies trying to be their best at that, they strive and strain to be something they can't be, doing something that will never fulfill them. Our prayers can block this plan of the Enemy and give our children a clear vision of themselves and their future.

From the time my children were small I prayed for God to reveal to us what their gifts and talents are. Along with that I asked for wisdom as to how to best encourage, nurture, develop, and train them to be all God made them to be. Helping them to appreciate their strengths and not dwell on their weaknesses was part of that; and since this wasn't easy during their teen years, it was a frequent focus of my prayers.

The biggest part of helping my son and daughter understand who God created them to be was encouraging their relationship with the Lord. I know they will never fully understand who *they* are until they understand who *God* is.

In the Bible where God promises to pour out His Spirit on our children, He says of them, "They will spring up among the grass like willows by the watercourses. One will say, 'I am the Lord's'; another will write with his hand, 'The Lord's'" (Isaiah 44:4–5). These children will know who they are. They will be filled with His Spirit and have that inner confidence of knowing they are His. You will see a confident and radiant expression on the face of any child who can say with conviction, "I am the Lord's." Do you want that for your child enough to pray for it?

PRAYER

Lord,

I pray that You would pour out Your Spirit upon (name of child) this day and anoint him (her) for all that You've called him (her) to be and do. Lord, You have said, "Let each one remain with God in that state in which he was called" (1 Corinthians 7:24). May it be for this child according to Your Word, that he (she) never stray from what You have called him (her) to be and do, or try to be something he (she) is not.

Deliver him (her) from any evil plan of the Devil to rob him (her) of life, to steal away his (her) uniqueness and giftedness, to compromise the path you've called him (her) to walk, or to destroy the person You created him (her) to be. May he (she) not be a follower of anyone but You, but may he (she) be a leader of people into Your kingdom. Help him (her) to grow into a complete understanding of his (her) authority in Jesus, while retaining a submissive and humble spirit. May the fruit of the Spirit, which is love, joy, peace, patience, kindness, goodness, faithfulness, gentleness, and self-control grow in him (her) daily (Galatians 5:22). May he (she) find his (her) identity in You, view himself (herself) as Your instrument, and know that he (she) is complete in You. Give him (her) a vision for his (her) life when setting goals for the future and a sense of purpose about what You've called him (her) to do. Help him (her) to see himself (herself) as You do—from his (her) future and not from his (her) past. May he (she) be convinced that Your thoughts toward him (her) are thoughts of peace and not of evil, to give him (her) a future and a hope (Jeremiah 29:11). Teach him (her) to look to You as his (her) hope for the future. May he (she) understand it is You "who has saved us and called us with a holy calling, not according to our works, but according to His own purpose and grace which was given to us in Christ Jesus before time began" (2 Timothy 1:9). May his (her) commitment to being who You created him (her) to be enable him (her) to grow daily in confidence and Holy Spirit boldness.

WEAPONS OF WARFARE

You are a chosen generation, a royal priesthood, a holy nation, His own special people, that you may proclaim the praises of Him who called you out of darkness into His marvelous light.
1 Peter 2:9

Eye has not seen, nor ear heard, nor have entered into the heart of man the things which God has prepared for those who love Him.
1 Corinthians 2:9

Be even more diligent to make your calling and
election sure, for if you do these things you
will never stumble.
2 PETER 1:10

We know that all things work together for good to
those who love God, to those who are the called
according to His purpose. For whom He foreknew,
He also predestined to be conformed to the image
of His Son, that He might be the firstborn among
many brethren. Moreover whom He predestined,
these He also called; whom He called, these
He also justified; and whom He justified,
these He also glorified.
ROMANS 8:28–30

Arise, shine; for your light has come! and the
glory of the Lord is risen upon you.
ISAIAH 60:1

CHAPTER ELEVEN

Following Truth, Rejecting Lies

In our house, our children know that while it might be possible to cut a deal on the punishment for certain infractions, if lying is part of the offense, the punishment will be swift, immediate, unpleasant, and non-negotiable. We consider telling a lie to be the worst offense because it is foundational for all other evil acts. Every sin or crime begins with someone believing or speaking a lie. Even if the lie is as simple as "I can get what I want if I lie," it paves the way for evil.

Early on, my daughter tested the water with "little white lies." But it didn't take long for her to see that the punishment for lying greatly overshadowed any possible advantage she thought she might gain as a result of telling a lie. My son, on the other hand, didn't just dabble. If he was going to tell a lie, he went for a big one.

When Christopher was seven, he was playing baseball with his friend Steven out in front of Steven's house. The ball struck the large front picture window with a loud crack, which immediately brought Steven's mother to the front door.

"Who did this?" she asked.

"I didn't do it," said Steven.

"I didn't do it," said Christopher.

"Steven, you mean to tell me you did not strike the window with this ball?" she said.

"No, I didn't," answered Steven emphatically.

"Christopher, did *you* strike the window with the ball?" she asked.

"If you saw me do it, I did it. If you didn't see me do it, I didn't do it," Christopher answered in his most matter-of-fact voice.

"I didn't see you do it," she said.

"Then I didn't do it," he replied.

When Steven's mom told us what happened, we knew we needed to deal with this matter immediately so Christopher would not think he could get away with lying.

"Christopher, someone saw everything that happened. Would you like to tell us about it?" I said, wanting his full confession and a repentant heart.

He hung his head and said, "Okay, I did it."

We had a long talk about what the Word of God says about lying. "Satan is a liar," I told him. "All the evil he does begins with a lie. People who lie believe that lying will make things better for them. But actually, it does just the opposite. That's because telling a lie means you have aligned yourself with Satan. Every time you lie you give Satan a piece of your heart. The more lies you tell, the more you give place in your heart to Satan's lying spirit, until eventually you can't stop yourself from lying. The Bible says, "Getting treasures by a lying tongue is the fleeting fantasy of those who seek death" (Proverbs 21:6). In other words, you may *think* you're getting something by lying, but all you're really doing is bringing death into your life. The consequences of telling the truth have to be better than death. Even the punishment you receive from your parents for lying will be far more pleasant than the consequences of lying. For the Bible promises that "A false witness will not go unpunished, and he who speaks lies will not escape" (Proverbs 19:5).

It was quite some time after that incident before Christopher asked me who had seen him that day.

"It was God," I explained. "He saw you. I've always asked Him to reveal to me anything I need to know about you or your sister. He is the Spirit of Truth, you understand."

"Mom, that's not fair," was all he said. After that, though, on the few occasions when he told a lie, he always came to me immediately to confess it.

"I thought I better tell you before you heard it from God," he would explain.

Children will lie at one time or another. The question is not *if* they will, but whether or not lying will become something they believe they can get away with. How we handle their lying will determine the outcome. If we don't teach our children what God says about lying, they won't know why it's wrong. If we don't discipline them when they lie, they will think that lying has no consequence. If we don't pray about this issue now, there will be bigger issues to deal with later.

The Bible says of the Devil, "He was a murderer from the beginning, and does not stand in the truth, because there is no truth in him. When he speaks a lie, he speaks from his own resources, for he is a liar and the father of it" (John 8:44). When you consider the source, there is no way you can sit by and allow the seed of a lie to take root in your child's heart.

Pray now that any lying spirit will be uprooted—not only in your children, but in *yourself* as well. Sometimes parents are soft on this subject with their children because they lie themselves. We need to reject the way of lying and follow the truth. We need to be an example to our children. *We* want to be able to say as John did, "I have no greater joy than to hear that my children walk in truth" (3 John 1:4). We don't want our children to be aligned with the father of lies. *We* want them to be aligned with the Father of Lights (James 1:17).

PRAYER

$\mathcal{L}$*ord,*

I pray that You will fill (name of child) with Your Spirit of truth. Give her (him) a heart that loves truth and follows after it, rejecting all lies as a manifestation of the Enemy. Flush out anything in her (him) that would entertain a lying spirit and cleanse her (him) from any death that has crept in as a result of lies she (he) may have spoken or thought. Help her (him) to understand that every lie gives the Devil a piece of her (his) heart, and into the hole that's left comes confusion, death, and separation from Your presence. Deliver her (him) from any lying spirit. I pray that she (he) not be blinded or deceived, but always be able to clearly understand Your truth.

I pray that she (he) will never be able to get away with lying—that all lies will come to light and be exposed. If she (he) lies, may she (he) be so miserable that confession and its consequences will seem like a relief. Help me to teach her (him) what it means to lie, and effectively discipline her (him) when she (he) tests that principle. Your Word says that "when He, the Spirit of truth, has come, He will guide you into all truth" (John 16:13). I pray that Your Spirit of truth will guide her (him) into all truth. May she (he) never be a person who gives place to lies, but rather a person of integrity who follows hard after the Spirit of truth.

WEAPONS OF WARFARE

Lying lips are an abomination to the Lord, but those who deal truthfully are His delight.
PROVERBS 12:22

My soul melts from heaviness; strengthen me according to Your Word. Remove from me the way of lying, and grant me Your law graciously.
PSALM 119:28–29

Let not mercy and truth forsake you; bind them around your neck, write them on the tablet of your heart, and so find favor and high esteem in the sight of God and man.
PROVERBS 3:3–4

The coming of the lawless one is according to the working of Satan, with all power, signs, and lying wonders, and with all unrighteous deception among those who perish, because they did not receive the love of the truth, that they might be saved.
2 THESSALONIANS 2:9–10

If you love Me, keep My commandments. And I will pray the Father, and He will give you another Helper, that He may abide with you forever—the Spirit of truth, whom the world cannot receive, because it neither sees Him nor knows Him; but you know Him, for He dwells with you and will be in you.
JOHN 14:15–17

CHAPTER TWELVE

Enjoying a Life of Health and Healing

When my daughter was four years old she was diagnosed with an eye problem which the doctor said would require her to have surgery and wear thick glasses for the rest of her life.

"Lord, is this what You have for my daughter?" I prayed. "Show me if it is because I don't have any peace about it."

My husband felt as I did, so we prayed for Amanda's eyes to be healed. We also prayed that, if necessary, we would find another doctor who could help her. The next day, seemingly out of nowhere, I received a call from someone who had no idea about Amanda's situation, but had information about an excellent specialist in the eye clinic at Children's Hospital in Los Angeles. I took Amanda to see this doctor, and after he thoroughly tested her, he offered encouraging news. He believed that contact lenses would correct the problem and she wouldn't have to have surgery. We felt immediate peace about his diagnosis and placed Amanda in this doctor's care, although we never stopped praying for her healing.

For eight years she wore contact lenses under the doctor's strict supervision. We did tire of putting her contacts in every morning and taking them out every night, and I wearied of having to run to school each time she lost one on the playground. But we persevered. Then one day when she was twelve years old, she went for her regular eye exam and the doctor said, "You no longer need contacts, glasses, or surgery. Your eyes are fine." We were ecstatic and so very grateful to God for His direction and His answer to prayer.

We have prayed our children through every cold, flu, fever, and injury, and the Lord has always answered. We never hesitate to take them to a doctor when they need it, of course, because we know God heals through doctors, too. But the Bible says, "Is anyone among you sick? Let him call for the elders of the church, and let them pray over him, anointing him with oil in the name of the Lord. And the prayer of faith will save the sick, and the Lord will raise him up" (James 5:14–15). The point is to pray first and see a doctor whenever necessary. And then, when we are healed, we are not to question or doubt.

After our son was in the car accident which I related earlier in this book, his back and knees were very sore. We, of course, prayed immediately for his healing and made sure he was x-rayed and checked thoroughly at the hospital. We continued to pray for complete healing, however, because we did not want him to have weakness in his back and knees that could be a problem for the rest of his life. When the insurance company for the driver of the other car, who was at fault in the accident, called to settle their responsibility, I felt *strongly* impressed by the Scripture, " 'For I will restore health to you and heal you of your wounds,' says the Lord" (Jeremiah 30:17). I was certain that my son was healed and that we were to refuse any compensation whatsoever. It was as if I heard God say, "Do you want the money or do you want the healing?"

"I want the healing, Lord, and thank You," I answered without hesitation.

I'm not saying that it is a lack of faith to collect insurance. I don't believe that at all. But in this instance refusing compensation was the right thing for us to do. When we pray for healing and God heals, we shouldn't act like it didn't happen.

The Bible is full of healing promises. David said, "Bless the Lord, O my soul, and forget not all His benefits: who forgives all your iniquities, who heals all your diseases" (Psalm 103:2–3). One of the main things Jesus wants to be to us is the forgiver of our sins and the healer of our bodies. Let's lay hold of the health and healing He has for our children by praying for it even *before* the need arises.

PRAYER

$\mathcal{L}ord,$

Because You have instructed us in Your Word
that we are to pray for one another so that we may
be healed, I pray for healing and wholeness for

(name of child). I pray that sickness and infirmity will have no place or power in his (her) life. I pray for protection against any disease coming into his (her) body. Your Word says, "He sent His word and healed them, and delivered them from their destructions" (Psalm 107:20). Wherever there is disease, illness, or infirmity in his (her) body, I pray that You, Lord, would touch him (her) with Your healing power and restore him (her) to total health.

Deliver him (her) from any destruction or injury that could come upon him (her). Specifically I ask You to heal (name any specific problem). If we are to see a doctor, I pray that You, Lord, would show us who that should be. Give that doctor wisdom and full knowledge of the best way to proceed.

Thank You, Lord, that You suffered and died for us so that we might be healed. I lay claim to that heritage of healing which You have promised in Your Word and provided for those who believe. I look to You for a life of health, healing, and wholeness for my child.

WEAPONS OF WARFARE

He was wounded for our transgressions, He was bruised for our iniquities; the chastisement for our peace was upon Him, and by His stripes we are healed.

ISAIAH 53:5

Confess your trespasses to one another, and pray for
one another, that you may be healed. The effective,
fervent prayer of a righteous man avails much.
JAMES 5:16

But to you who fear My name the Sun of Righteousness shall arise with healing in His wings.
MALACHI 4:2

For to this you were called, because Christ also
suffered for us, leaving us an example, that you
should follow His steps . . . who Himself bore our
sins in His own body on the tree, that we, having
died to sins, might live for righteousness—by
whose stripes you were healed.
1 PETER 2:22,24

Your light shall break forth like the morning, your
healing shall spring forth speedily, and your
righteousness shall go before you; the glory
of the Lord shall be your rear guard.
ISAIAH 58:8

CHAPTER THIRTEEN

Having the Motivation for Proper Body Care

Left to themselves in this junk-food world, children will be attracted to all the wrong foods. Much of what we eat has been so masked, processed, stripped, altered, added to, and taken away from, that it has little food value. But children don't care about that. They just want food that looks good, smells good, tastes good— and if they've seen it advertised on TV that's even better. And if you have a spouse, as I do, who loves junk food and brings it into the house for himself and the children, you have an even more difficult situation. I knew I was in trouble the day I came home, after leaving our ten-month-old son with his father for the afternoon, and found carbonated cola in his baby bottle. I realized then that prayer was my only hope.

I did my best to make healthy meals desirable, and I tried to teach my children proper eating habits. I was even willing to endure criticism from them.

"I hate this. We're the only people in the world who don't have any junk food in their kitchen," said my son in utter disgust.

"We're so healthy it makes me sick," said my daughter with tears in her eyes.

Because I believe that "better is a dry morsel with quietness, than a house full of feasting with strife" (Proverbs 17:1), I haven't made an issue of this nearly as much as I would like. I know I can't force my children to make healthful food choices when I'm not around to remind them. Only the power of God through prayer can make the difference.

Nearly everyone struggles somewhat in the area of proper body care. But because of the health books I've written and the exercise videos I've made, I have come in contact with countless people who seriously battle with this issue—even to the point of heartbreaking agony and defeat. We do our children a disservice if we don't support them in prayer, as well as guide and instruct them in healthy practices, so that they don't end up with this kind of misery.

If your children are young, start praying for them to be attracted to healthful food and to desire to exercise and take good care of their bodies. If you don't, by the time they are in their teens, they may have already developed bad habits and the situation can quickly get out of control. We see this in the eating disorders that are epidemic among teen and college-age girls and which are now being seen more and more in boys. Start praying before any such symptoms appear.

If your children are older, begin right now to intercede on their behalf. Many young women who suffer with anorexia and bulimia struggle against more than just the desires of the flesh; they face a spiritual battle as well. They are bound to obsessive eating habits which are deadly and completely opposed to the way God created them to live. I have known far too many young women who suffer in this regard. The ones who have parents who learn to intercede on their behalf later have success stories to tell. Others less fortunate do not.

Your child needs Holy Spirit guidance and strength to do what's right for his or her body. Your prayers can spare them much defeat, frustration, and heartbreak. Don't you wish you'd had someone praying about this for you? I know I do.

PRAYER

Lord,
I lift (name of child) to You and ask that You would place in her (him) a desire to eat healthy food. I know that throughout her (his) life she (he) will be tempted to make poor food choices and eat that which brings death instead of life. Help her (him) to understand what's good for her (him) and what isn't, and give her (him) a desire for food that is healthful. Let her (him) be repulsed or dissatisfied with food that is harmful.

I pray that she (he) be spared from all eating disorders in any form. By the authority given me in Jesus Christ (Luke 10:19), on my daughter's (son's) behalf, I say "No to anorexia," "No to bulimia," "No to food addiction," "No to overeating," "No to starvation diets," "No to any kind of unbalanced eating habits."

Lord, Your Word says, "You shall know the truth, and the truth shall make you free" (John 8:32). Help her (him) to see the truth about the way she (he) is to live, so that she (he) can be set free from unhealthful habits. I pray that along with the desire to eat properly, You would give her (him) the motivation to exercise regularly, to drink plenty of pure water, and to control and manage stress in her (his) life by living according to Your Word. Whenever she (he) struggles in any of those areas may she (he) turn to You and say, "Teach me Your way, O LORD" (Psalm 27:11). Give her (him) a vision of her (his) body as the temple of Your Holy Spirit.

I pray that she (he) will value the body You've given her (him) and desire to take proper care of it. May she (he) not be critical of it, nor examine herself (himself) through the microscope of public opinion and acceptance. I pray that she (he) will not be bound by the lure of fashion magazines, television, or movies which try to influence her (him) with an image of what they say she (he) should look like. Enable her (him) to say, "Turn away my eyes from looking at worthless things" (Psalm 119:37). Help her (him) to see that what makes a person truly attractive is Your Holy Spirit living in her (him) and radiating outward. May she (he) come to understand that true attractiveness begins in the heart of one who loves God.

Establish *Your* vision of health and attractiveness in her (his) heart this day, and permanently instill in her (him) the desire to take proper care of her (his) body because it is the temple of your Holy Spirit.

WEAPONS OF WARFARE

Do you not know that your body is the temple of the Holy Spirit who is in you, whom you have from God, and you are not your own? For you were bought at a price; therefore glorify God in your body and in your spirit, which are God's.
1 CORINTHIANS 6:19–20

If anyone defiles the temple of God, God will destroy him. For the temple of God is holy, which temple you are.
1 CORINTHIANS 3:17

I beseech you therefore, brethren, by the mercies of God, that you present your bodies a living sacrifice, holy, acceptable to God, which is your reasonable service.
ROMANS 12:1

Put on the Lord Jesus Christ, and make no
provision for the flesh, to fulfill its lusts.
ROMANS 13:14

Therefore, whether you eat or drink, or whatever
you do, do all to the glory of God.
1 CORINTHIANS 10:31

CHAPTER FOURTEEN

Instilling the Desire to Learn

School was a frightening experience for me socially, but getting A's was easy. That's why I never thought to pray about my children having the ability or the motivation to learn. That is, until it became clear that one of my children had a form of dyslexia. Because this child was bright, intelligent, and exceptionally gifted, the possibility of a learning difficulty never crossed my mind. However, school was a struggle from the beginning, and we didn't understand what was happening until our child's learning difficulty was professionally diagnosed in the third grade. Although there have been many heartbreaking moments because of this problem, prayer has sustained us along the way. My husband and I and our prayer partners continue to pray that this child will either be totally healed or be completely at peace about it and accept it as part of our child's wonderful uniqueness.

In one way or another, of course, we all have deficiencies. Thankfully, God makes up for our deficiencies with His strength. His Word says, "Not that we are sufficient of ourselves to think of anything as being from ourselves, but our sufficiency is from God" (2 Corinthians 3:5). That is so true. God has gotten our child through each year of school successfully, and through the process, we are all learning that true knowledge and understanding begin with and come from the Lord.

The Bible teaches us that knowledge begins with a reverence for God and His ways. If we receive His words and treasure His commands in our heart, if we work at trying to understand and ask God to help us do so, if we seek understanding as fervently as we would search out hidden treasure, then we will find the knowledge of God (Proverbs 2:1–12). And what a vast knowledge it is. So grand, in fact, it is a shield that delivers and protects us from evil.

A child's ability and desire to learn cannot be taken for granted. Even while our child is still in the womb we can pray, "Lord, let this child be knit perfectly together with a good, strong, healthy mind and body and be taught by You forever." The earlier we start praying the better, of course, but no matter what age your child is, your prayers will make a positive and permanent difference.

PRAYER

Lord,

I pray that (name of child) will have a deep reverence for You and Your ways. May he (she) hide Your Word in his (her) heart like a treasure, and seek after understanding like silver or gold. Give him (her) a good mind, a teachable spirit, and an ability to learn. Instill in him (her) a *desire* to attain knowledge and skill, and may he (she) have *joy* in the process. Above all, I pray that he (she) will be taught by You, for Your Word says that when our children are taught by You they are guaranteed peace. You have also said, "The fear of the Lord is the beginning of knowledge, but fools despise wisdom and instruction" (Proverbs 1:7). May he (she) never be a fool and turn away from learning, but rather may he (she) turn to You for the knowledge he (she) needs.

I pray he (she) will respect the wisdom of his (her) parents and be willing to be taught by them. May he (she) also have the desire to be taught by the teachers You bring into his (her) life. Handpick each one, Lord, and may they be godly people from whom he (she) can easily learn. Take out of his (her) life any teacher who would be an ungodly influence or create a bad learning experience. Let him (her) find favor with his (her) teachers and have good communication with them. Help him (her) to excel in school and do well in any classes he (she) may take. Make the pathways of learning smooth and not something with which he (she) must strain and struggle. Connect everything in his (her) brain the way it is supposed to be so that he (she) has clarity of thought, organization, good memory, and strong learning ability.

I say to him (her) according to Your Word, "Apply your heart to instruction, and your ears to words of knowledge" (Proverbs 23:12). "May the Lord give you understanding in all things" (2 Timothy 2:7). Lord, enable him (her) to experience the joy of learning more about You and Your world.

WEAPONS OF WARFARE

All your children shall be taught by the Lord, and
great shall be the peace of your children.
ISAIAH 54:13

A wise man will hear and increase learning, and a
man of understanding will attain wise counsel.
PROVERBS 1:5

My people are destroyed for lack of knowledge.
Because you have rejected knowledge, I also will
reject you from being priest for Me; because you
have forgotten the law of your God, I also will
forget your children.
HOSEA 4:6

Take firm hold of instruction, do not let go;
keep her, for she is your life.
PROVERBS 4:13

My son, if you receive my words, and treasure my
commands within you, so that you incline your ear to
wisdom, and apply your heart to understanding; yes, if
you cry out for discernment, and lift up your voice for
understanding, if you seek her as silver, and search for
her as for hidden treasures; then you will understand
the fear of the LORD, and find the knowledge of God.
PROVERBS 2:1–5

CHAPTER FIFTEEN

Identifying God-Given Gifts and Talents

From the time my children were born, I prayed for God to reveal to us the gifts, talents, and abilities He had placed in them and to show us how to best nurture and develop them for His glory. At a very early age both of our children showed signs of musical talent, so I asked God what to do about it and waited on Him for the answer.

When Christopher was four, we felt directed to give him piano lessons. He showed remarkable ability, but after a couple of years did not want to practice. God gave me clear indication, however, that I would not be a good steward of the gifts He had given my son if I let him stop at that point. So I devised an appropriate incentive for my six-year-old: I would pay him twenty-five cents every time he practiced. This payment plan must have been Holy Spirit inspired, because I never heard another complaint about practicing until Christopher was twelve. At that time I felt released to let him stop studying piano and start taking the drum lessons he wanted. And I've never had to ask him to practice drums. In fact, quite the opposite!

Today Christopher performs on electric keyboards, drums, bass, and guitar, but he writes all his songs and arrangements on the piano. His music instructors say that he does so well because his knowledge of piano has given him a good foundational understanding of music, which only confirms God's leading all those years ago.

I've sensed the same Holy Spirit leading for my daughter with regard to her singing ability. Because the Enemy wants to use our children's gifts for *his* glory, or at the very least keep them from being used for God's purposes, we need to cover them in prayer. Praying for the development of our children's God-given gifts and talents is an ongoing process.

There was a time in both of my children's lives— between the ages of twelve and fourteen—when they were attracted to the world's music and the unacceptable appearance and behavior of certain popular artists. My husband and I knew our battle was with the Devil, not with our children, but we also knew we had to confront them about the matter and establish rules about what music they could listen to and what was unacceptable. (This does not mean that we think our children should never have anything at all to do with secular music. But whatever they do, they must "do all to the glory of God" [1 Corinthians 10:31] because God has called them to do it.)

We prayed our children's eyes would be turned away from the world and focused on what God had called them to do. We prayed that *God* would *open the doors* they were to go through and *shut all doors* that they were not to enter. We've seen Him answer that prayer many times. For example, Christopher was asked to be a part of a number of different musical groups and tour with them on the road. We never felt peace about any of them being the right situation or timing for *him.* Then, when he was eighteen, he was offered the opportunity to produce, write, arrange, and play keyboards, bass, and drums on a worship album for Sparrow Records. We knew this was clearly from the Lord and an answer to our prayers concerning his talents being used for God's glory. This does not end our prayers in this regard, of course. My husband and I are well aware of what the music business is like and the temptations of road life, even for Christian artists, so we will continue to pray for Christopher's faithfulness to use his talents and life for God's glory.

What gifts and talents has God planted in *your* child? Every child has them. They are there, whether you can see them or not. The Bible says, "Each one has his own gift from God, one in this manner and another in that" (1 Corinthians 7:7). Sometimes it takes prayer to uncover them.

When God gives you a glimpse of your child's potential for greatness, love and pray him (her) into being that. The Bible says, "Do you see a man who excels in his work? He will stand before kings; he will not stand before unknown men" (Proverbs 22:29). Pray that your child will develop and excel in the gifts and talents God has given him (her), and let him (her) know he (she) has a unique purpose and significance in this world.

Each child has special gifts and talents. We need to pray for them to be identified, revealed, developed, nurtured, and used for God's glory.

PRAYER

Lord,

I thank You for the gifts and talents You have placed in (name of child). I pray that You would develop them in her (him) and use them for Your glory. Make them apparent to me and to her (him), and show me specifically if there is any special nurturing, training, learning experience, or opportunities I should provide for her (him). May her (his) gifts and talents be developed in Your way and in Your time.

Your Word says, "Having then gifts differing according to the grace that is given to us, let us use them" (Romans 12:6). As she (he) recognizes the talents and abilities You've given her (him), I pray that no feelings of inadequacy, fear, or uncertainty will keep her (him) from using them according to Your will. May she (he) hear the call You have on her (his) life so that she (he) doesn't spend a lifetime trying to figure out what it is or miss it altogether. Let her (his) talent never be wasted, watered down by mediocrity, or used to glorify anything or anyone other than You, Lord.

I pray that You would reveal to her (him) what her (his) life work is to be and help her (him) excel in it. Bless the work of her (his) hands, and may she (he) be able to earn a good living doing the work she (he) loves and does best.

Your Word says that, "A man's gift makes room for him, and brings him before great men" (Proverbs 18:16). May whatever she (he) does find favor with others and be well received and respected. But most of all, I pray the gifts and talents You placed in her (him) be released to find their fullest expression in glorifying You.

WEAPONS OF WARFARE

For the gifts and the calling of God are irrevocable.
ROMANS 11:29

To each one of us grace was given according to the measure of Christ's gift.
EPHESIANS 4:7

As each one has received a gift, minister it to one another, as good stewards of the manifold grace of God.
1 PETER 4:10

Every good gift and every perfect gift is from above,
and comes down from the Father of lights, with whom
there is no variation or shadow of turning.
JAMES 1:17

I thank my God always concerning you for the grace of
God which was given to you by Christ Jesus, that you
were enriched in everything by Him in all utterance
and all knowledge, even as the testimony of Christ
was confirmed in you, so that you come short in
no gift, eagerly waiting for the revelation of
our Lord Jesus Christ.
1 CORINTHIANS 1:4–7

CHAPTER SIXTEEN

Learning to Speak Life

After school one afternoon I heard my son say a couple of swear words.

"That kind of language is not acceptable," I told him. "Why are you using those words when you know you shouldn't?"

"The kids at school talk that way," he explained.

"Other people do it, so it's okay for you?" I questioned. Then in my next sentence I rattled off a string of four-letter words I used to say before I met the Lord and was refined by His Spirit.

With a look of horror and shock he exclaimed, "Mom! Why are you talking like that?"

"Other people talk that way," I said. "How does it make you feel when I talk like that?"

"It makes me feel awful."

"You know, I can talk like that any time I want. But I choose *not* to. When I say those words it makes you feel bad because it hurts your spirit. When *you* talk like that, it hurts *my* spirit. Imagine what it does to God's Spirit. You have a choice whether to grieve *God's* Spirit with the words you say or to glorify Him. He'll love you either way and so will I. But one way will bless and one way will hurt."

I didn't hear Christopher say any words like that again until he was a teenager. Then we had this conversation all over again. I pray to this day he will remember it.

I know my teaching method may seem shocking. It shocked me, too, and I asked God to cleanse me from the contamination I felt for even speaking those words. But those words did not come from my heart. I said them only as a means of demonstrating their destructiveness. I'm not recommending that you adopt my methods of teaching, but that you accept my experience as a valid example of the power of what we speak.

We create a world for ourselves by what we speak. Words have power, and we can either speak life or death into a situation. The Bible says that what we say can get us *into* trouble or keep us *away* from it. It can even save our lives. "He who guards his mouth preserves his life, but he who opens wide his lips shall have destruction" (Proverbs 13:3). We need to ask God to put a guard over our own mouth as well as the mouth of our child.

Speech that is not godly or not of the Lord, such as, "I'm no good," "I wish I was dead," "Life is terrible," "People are horrible," "I'll never be anything special," does not reflect a heart filled with the Holy Spirit. It reflects the work of darkness. And that is exactly what will play itself out on the stage of your child's life if you don't help him monitor what he says.

The Bible says that when we go to be with the Lord we will have to account for every careless word we have spoken. We pay for them here on earth also. I believe the price is too high to pay for something that can easily be controlled by our own will. We can speak love, joy, and peace into our world, or we can speak strife, hatred, deception, and all other manifestations of evil.

We want our children to speak life. This doesn't mean they can't be honest about negative feelings. But those words should be spoken for the purpose of confession, understanding, and submission to God for healing, not as tools of destruction.

When our children's words reflect negatively on themselves, others, their situation, or the world around them, we must encourage them to see in God's Word all that could be better said. The best way to improve speech is to improve the heart, "For out of the abundance of the heart the mouth speaks" (Matthew 12:34). A heart filled with the Holy Spirit and the truth of the Word of God will produce godly speech that brings life to the speaker as well as the listener. This is where our point of prayer should begin.

PRAYER

Lord,

I pray that (name of child) will choose to use speech that glorifies You. Fill his (her) heart with Your Spirit and Your truth so that what overflows from his (her) mouth will be words of life and not death. Put a monitor over his (her) mouth so that every temptation to use profane, negative, cruel, hurtful, uncaring, unloving, or compassionless language would pierce his (her) spirit and make him (her) feel uncomfortable. I pray that obscene or foul language be so foreign to him (her) that if words like that ever do find their way through his (her) lips, they will be like gravel in his (her) mouth and he (she) will be repulsed by them. Help him (her) to hear himself (herself) so that words don't come out carelessly or thoughtlessly.

Keep him (her) from being snared by the words of his (her) mouth. You've promised that "whoever guards his mouth and tongue keeps his soul from troubles" (Proverbs 21:23). Help him (her) to put a guard over his (her) mouth and keep far away from adversity. Your Word says that "Death and life are in the power of the tongue, and those who love it will eat its fruit" (Proverbs 18:21). May he (she) speak life and not death. May he (she) be quick to listen and slow to speak so that his (her) speech will always be seasoned with grace. Equip him (her) to know how, what, and when to speak to anyone in any

situation. Enable him (her) to always speak
words of hope, health, encouragement, and life,
and to resolve that his (her) mouth will not sin.

WEAPONS OF WARFARE

Let the words of my mouth and the meditation of
my heart be acceptable in Your sight, O LORD,
my strength and my redeemer.
PSALM 19:14

A good man out of the good treasure of his heart
brings forth good things, and an evil man out of
the evil treasure brings forth evil things.
MATTHEW 12:35

But I say to you that for every idle word men may
speak, they will give account of it in the day of
judgment. For by your words you will be justified,
and by your words you will be condemned.
MATTHEW 12:36–37

Pleasant words are like a honeycomb, sweetness
to the soul and health to the bones.
PROVERBS 16:24

There is one who speaks like the piercings of a sword,
but the tongue of the wise promotes health.
PROVERBS 12:18

CHAPTER SEVENTEEN

Staying Attracted to Holiness and Purity

Children who are taught to live in purity and holiness have distinctly radiant faces and a compelling attractiveness. The Bible says, "Even a child is known by his deeds, whether what he does is pure and right" (Proverbs 20:11). We want our children to be known for their goodness. We want our children to be attractive to others because of their purity. This doesn't just happen. It must be taught. And although we can do much to teach our children about living purely in the ways of the Lord and model this to the best of our ability, the real teacher is the Holy Spirit. Holiness begins with a love for Him. "Keep yourself pure" (1 Timothy 5:22), the Bible instructs us. That's a hard assignment for anyone, but especially for a child. It can only be accomplished by total submission to God and His law and the enabling power of the Holy Spirit.

When my son started his senior year in high school, he was at a new school, in a different state, and in a different culture—a tough assignment for any young person, no matter how grounded or godly. The school he attended was a small private Christian school, so within the first week he had met all the senior boys. One of the young men stood out, however. His name was Sandy, and he was a sports star, excelled in his studies, and had received award after award for outstanding achievement. But Sandy was outstanding in another, more important way: his words and his actions reflected his deep respect for God and His laws.

One day at lunch when all the guys were together, one of them told an off-color joke and everyone laughed. Everyone, that is, except Sandy. My son admitted that he laughed, too.

"I was the new guy and I didn't want everyone to think I was from another planet," he sheepishly explained when he told us about it later.

What Christopher soon came to realize was that Sandy never laughed at obscene humor. Nor did he smoke or drink or use bad language. Yet, amazingly, everyone liked and respected him.

One day, shortly after a parents' meeting at the school, I came home and told Christopher about a wonderful woman I had met there.

"She stands out," I told him. "She's very warm and loving—a godly woman with a wonderful sense of humor. And she made me feel so welcome, like I've known her forever." As I went on to describe her, I mentioned her name.

"That's Sandy's mother," he said.

"Of course," I replied. "I should have known that Sandy would have strong, exceptional, believing, and praying parents. No child turns out like that by accident."

Throughout Christopher's senior year we observed that whole family and saw how exceptional each member was; and we noticed that people were not turned off by their goodness. Why? Because the way they lived was not a legalistic attempt to be perfect or to impress others; it was done from hearts that had a deep reverence for God and a desire to live His way—in holiness and purity.

My son is no longer at that school and we don't see Sandy or his family any more because our lives have gone different directions. But we will never forget them. They raised our personal standards, gave us something higher to aim for, and allowed us to see how attractive holiness is.

Let's pray for our children to be attracted to holiness and purity like a magnet, so that when anything entices them that isn't holy or pure, they detect the pull immediately and are made uncomfortable enough to thoroughly reject it. "For God did not call us to uncleanness, but to holiness" (1 Thessalonians 4:7). To live purely within the boundaries of God's law is to find wholeness in the total person. That wholeness is what holiness is all about. Children who have a desire for holiness and seek God's enabling power to help them achieve it can never be anything but blessed and fulfilled.

Sandy exemplified the Scripture that says, "Let no one despise your youth, but be an example to the believers in word, in conduct, in love, in spirit, in faith, in purity" (1 Timothy 4:12). There is nothing more compelling than children who walk in holiness and purity. Let's pray for our children to be among those who do.

PRAYER

Lord,

I pray that You would fill (name of child) with a love for You that surpasses her (his) love for anything or anyone else. Help her (him) to respect and revere Your laws and understand that they are there for her (his) benefit. May she (he) clearly see that when Your laws are disobeyed, life doesn't work. Hide Your Word in her (his) heart so that there is no attraction to sin. I pray she (he) will run from evil, from impurity, from unholy thoughts, words, and deeds, and that she (he) will be drawn toward whatever is pure and holy. Let Christ be formed in her (him) and cause her (him) to seek the power of Your Holy Spirit to enable her (him) to do what is right.

You have said, "Blessed are the pure in heart, for they shall see God" (Matthew 5:8). May a desire for holiness that comes from a pure heart be reflected in all that she (he) does. Let it be manifested in her (his) appearance as well. I pray that the clothes she (he) wears and the way she (he) styles her (his) hair and chooses to adorn her (his) body and face will reflect a reverence and a desire to glorify You, Lord.

Where she (he) has strayed from the path of holiness, bring her (him) to repentance and work Your cleansing power in her (his) heart and life. Give her (him) understanding that to live in purity brings wholeness and blessing, and that the greatest reward for it is seeing You.

WEAPONS OF WARFARE

Who may ascend into the hill of the Lord? Or who may stand in His holy place? He who has clean hands and a pure heart, who has not lifted up his soul to an idol, nor sworn deceitfully. He shall receive blessing from the Lord, and righteousness from the God of his salvation.
PSALM 24:3–5

In a great house there are not only vessels of gold and silver, but also of wood and clay, some for honor and some for dishonor. Therefore if anyone cleanses himself from the latter, he will be a vessel for honor, sanctified and useful for the Master, prepared for every good work.
2 TIMOTHY 2:20–21

Every branch in me that does not bear fruit He takes away; and every branch that bears fruit He prunes, that it may bear more fruit.
JOHN 15:2

A highway shall be there, and a road, and it shall be
called the Highway of Holiness. The unclean shall not
pass over it, but it shall be for others. Whoever walks
the road, although a fool, shall not go astray . . . the
redeemed shall walk there, and the ransomed of the
Lord shall return, and come to Zion with singing, with
everlasting joy on their heads. They shall obtain joy
and gladness, and sorrow and sighing shall flee away.
ISAIAH 35:8–10

There is a generation that is pure in its own eyes,
yet is not washed from its filthiness.
PROVERBS 30:12

CHAPTER EIGHTEEN

Praying Through a Child's Room

When my son was about eleven, he suddenly started having nightmares for no apparent reason. He hadn't seen anything frightening in a movie or on TV, and he gave us no indication that anything out of the ordinary had happened to him. We prayed with him several times, but night after night the bad dreams persisted.

As I was praying alone about this one morning, I asked God to show me what was causing these nightmares. As I did, I felt strongly led to go to my son's room.

"Lord, if there is anything in Christopher's room that shouldn't be here, show me," I prayed. Immediately, I felt prompted to go to his computer and look at his games. The first game I picked up was one he had borrowed from a friend at church. The outside of the box looked totally harmless; it was just a boy's action-adventure game. I opened the box and pulled out the small instruction booklet. The first few pages revealed nothing unusual, but in the back pages I found the worst kind of satanic garbage. I was shocked, but I said, "Thank you, Jesus," and took the game out of his room immediately.

If the game had been my son's property, I would have destroyed it immediately. But since it belonged to someone else, I called the boy's parents and told them what I had found. They were as surprised and unaware as we had been. When Christopher got home from school, I showed him what I had discovered. He said he hadn't gotten that far in the game yet and didn't realize what was in it. He had no hesitation about giving it back.

When my husband came home, we anointed our son's room with oil and thoroughly prayed through it. We knew the Bible said, "The yoke will be destroyed because of the anointing oil" (Isaiah 10:27). And although most of the biblical examples of that are of people being anointed, there are also examples of buildings or rooms being anointed to sanctify them. "You shall take the anointing oil, and anoint the tabernacle and all that is in it; and you shall hallow it and all its utensils, and it shall be holy" (Exodus 40:9). Because we wanted to break any yoke of the Enemy and cleanse our son's room of anything unholy, we anointed the doorpost and prayed over his room, inviting the Holy Spirit to dwell there and crowd out anything that was not of God.

The proof to us that we had done the right thing was that Christopher's nightmares stopped immediately— just as suddenly as they began.

Everyone's house needs a spiritual housecleaning from time to time, especially in the rooms where our children sleep and play. The Bible says if we bring anything detestable into our homes, we bring destruction along with it. A holy housecleaning should be done periodically as a matter of principle, but definitely whenever you feel troubled by something in your child. If he or she is becoming fearful, rebellious, angry, depressed, distant, strange, a disciplinary problem, or having bad dreams and nightmares, sometimes simply praying through the room can change things quickly. Singing Christian songs, hymns, and worship choruses in the room is also very effective, and I've seen a change of spirit in my children after I have done so.

I know one mother and father who battled a heavy Enemy stronghold of alcohol, drugs, rebellion, and occult involvement in their sixteen-year-old son by playing Christian worship songs and the Word of God on tape in his room while he was at school. His rebelliousness was eventually broken and he became a peaceful and godly person.

When you pray through your child's room, remove anything that is not glorifying to God: posters, books, magazines, pictures, photos, games, or articles of clothing depicting drug or alcohol use or any kind of blasphemy. Of course God's Word on this should be lovingly explained to the child and, if at all possible, he should be encouraged to remove the offensive articles himself. Explain that for his own peace and blessing he must clean the room of anything that is not of the Lord. Then pray over the room thoroughly. I've seen miraculous transformations as a result of doing that.

This is not a superstitious little ritual. This is a powerful claiming of your home, your child, and all aspects of his life for God. It's standing up and proclaiming, "As for me and my house, we will serve the Lord" (Joshua 24:15). It's saying, "My home is sanctified and set apart for God's glory."

Let's start our spiritual housecleaning by praying through our children's rooms even *before* the need arises.

PRAYER

Lord,

I invite Your Holy Spirit to dwell in this room, which belongs to (name of child). You are Lord over heaven and earth, and I proclaim that You are Lord over this room as well. Flood it with Your light and life. Crowd out any darkness which seeks to impose itself here, and let no spirits of fear, depression, anger, doubt, anxiety, rebelliousness, or hatred (name anything you've seen manifested in your child's behavior) find any place here. I pray that nothing will come into this room that is not brought by You, Lord. If there is anything here that shouldn't be, show me so it can be taken out.

Put Your complete protection over this room so that evil cannot enter here by any means. Fill this room with Your love, peace, and joy. I pray that my child will say, as David did, "I will walk within my house with a perfect heart. I will set nothing wicked before my eyes" (Psalm 101:2–3). I pray that You, Lord, will make this room a holy place, sanctified for Your glory.

WEAPONS OF WARFARE

Nor shall you bring an abomination into your house,
lest you be doomed to destruction like it.
DEUTERONOMY 7:26

Wash yourselves, make yourselves clean; put away
the evil of your doings from before My eyes.
Cease to do evil.
ISAIAH 1:16

Therefore, having these promises, beloved, let us
cleanse ourselves from all filthiness of the flesh and
spirit, perfecting holiness in the fear of God.
2 CORINTHIANS 7:1

Have mercy upon me, O God, according to Your loving
kindness; according to the multitude of Your tender
mercies, blot out my transgressions. Wash me thoroughly from my iniquity, and cleanse me from my sin.
PSALM 51:1–2

The curse of the Lord is on the house of the wicked,
but He blesses the habitation of the just.
PROVERBS 3:33

CHAPTER NINETEEN

Enjoying Freedom from Fear

Fear was a way of life for me as a child because I lived with a mother who was mentally ill. Her bizarre, erratic, and abusive behavior was a constant source of terror. When, as an adult, I came to know the Lord, I learned to identify the *true* source of fear and battle against it. I've employed the same tactics on behalf of my children.

In Los Angeles we lived through earthquakes, fires, floods, riots, and rampant crime. Fear could have controlled our lives if we'd let it. In fact, we found ourselves praying about fear and protection so often that this plea became part of every prayer. Whenever I saw fear begin to grip either of my children, we would pray, read the Bible, sing hymns and worship choruses, and play Christian music. Since we moved away from that area we don't have to deal with that kind of fear on a daily basis anymore, but the lessons we learned about God's perfect love casting out all fear have been etched forever in each of our hearts.

112

Fear is something that comes upon us the moment we don't believe that God is able to keep us, or all we care about, safe. FEAR—or False Evidence Appearing Real—easily strikes children because they can't always discern what's real and what isn't. Our comfort, reassurance, and love can *help* them; but praying, speaking the Word of God in faith, and praising God for His love and power, can *free* them.

When Jesus was at sea with His disciples and a storm came up, He responded to their terror by saying, "Why are you fearful, O you of little faith" (Matthew 8:26). He wants us, like them, to believe that our boat won't sink if He's in it with us.

There are times, however, when fear is more than a passing emotion. It can grip a child's heart so strongly and so unreasonably that no actions or words can take it away. When that happens, the child is being harassed by a spirit of fear. And the Bible clearly tells us a spirit of fear does not come from God. It comes from the Enemy of our soul.

Parents have the authority and power through Jesus Christ to resist that spirit of fear on their child's behalf. *Fear* doesn't have power over *them*. *We* have power over *it*. Jesus gave us authority over *all* the power of the Enemy (Luke 10:19). Don't be deceived into thinking otherwise. If fear persists after you have prayed, ask two or more strong believers to pray with you. Where two or three are gathered together in the name of the Lord, He is there in the midst of them (Matthew 18:20). Fear and the presence of the Lord cannot occupy the same space.

Because we have Jesus, we and our children never have to live with or accept a spirit of fear as a way of life.

PRAYER

Lord,

Your Word says, "I sought the Lord, and He heard me, and delivered me from all my fears" (Psalm 34:4). I seek You this day, believing that You hear me, and I pray that You will deliver (name of child) from any fear that threatens to overtake her (him). You said You have "not given us a spirit of fear, but of power and of love and of a sound mind" (2 Timothy 1:7). Flood her (him) with Your love and wash away all fear and doubt. Give her (him) a sense of Your loving presence that far outweighs any fear that would threaten to overtake her (him). Help her (him) to rely on Your power in such a manner that it establishes strong confidence and faith in You. Give her (him) a mind so sound that she (he) can recognize any false evidence the Devil presents to her (him) and identify it as having no basis in reality.

Wherever there is real danger or good reason to fear, give her (him) wisdom, protect her (him), and draw her (him) close to You. Help her (him) not to deny her (his) fears, but take them to You in prayer and seek deliverance from them. I pray

that as she (he) draws close to You, Your love will
penetrate her (his) life and crowd out all fear.
Plant Your Word in her (his) heart. Let faith take
root in her (his) mind and soul as she (he) grows
in Your Word.

Thank You, Lord, for Your promise to deliver
us from all our fears. In Jesus' name I pray for
freedom from fear on behalf of my child this day.

WEAPONS OF WARFARE

Oh, how great is Your goodness, which You have laid
up for those who fear You, which You have prepared
for those who trust in You in the presence of
the sons of men!
PSALM 31:19

Fear not, for I am with you; be not dismayed, for I am
your God. I will strengthen you, yes, I will help you, I
will uphold you with My righteous right hand.
ISAIAH 41:10

He shall cover you with His feathers, and under His
wings you shall take refuge; His truth shall be your
shield and buckler. You shall not be afraid of the terror
by night, nor of the arrow that flies by day, nor of the
pestilence that walks in darkness, nor of the
destruction that lays waste at noonday.
PSALM 91:4–6

The Lord is my light and my salvation; whom shall I fear? The Lord is the strength of my life; of whom shall I be afraid?

PSALM 27:1

The pangs of death surrounded me, and the floods of ungodliness made me afraid. The sorrows of Sheol surrounded me; the snares of death confronted me. In my distress I called upon the Lord, and cried out to my God; He heard my voice from His temple, and my cry came before Him, even to His ears.

PSALM 18:4–6

There is no fear in love; but perfect love casts out fear, because fear involves torment. But he who fears has not been made perfect in love.

1 JOHN 4:18

CHAPTER TWENTY

Receiving a Sound Mind

The world and the Devil are making every effort to control your child's mind. The good news is that you have the authority to resist those efforts. If your child is young, you have authority over what he puts *into* his mind—the television, movies, and videos he watches, the radio programs, tapes, and CD's he listens to, the books and magazines he reads. You can also do much to help your child fill his mind with godly music, words, and pictures. But most important of all, you have the power of prayer. So, even if your child is beyond your daily influence, you can pray for his or her mind to be sound, protected, and freed.

One of the many wonderful things about receiving Jesus and being filled with the Holy Spirit is that along with every other blessing, we gain a stability and sound-mindedness that cannot be acquired any other way. That's because we are given the mind of Christ. The Bible says, "Let this mind be in you which was also in

Christ Jesus" (Philippians 2:5). We can resist the worldly mind and allow His mind to be in control, and we can continually renew our minds by taking every thought captive.

My mother suffered with mental illness from her early twenties until she died at age sixty-seven. I saw firsthand what it was like for someone to live in a fantasy world and have no control over the thoughts that came into her mind. It was a frightening experience. Once I came to know the Lord, I frequently prayed that neither my children nor I would inherit any of that mental instability. Whenever I felt concern I said, "For God has not given us a spirit of fear, but of power and of love and of a sound mind" (2 Timothy 1:7).

"God has given me a *sound mind*," I have said many times. "He has also given my son a sound mind and my daughter a sound mind. I will accept nothing less."

Mental illness does not have to be passed along from one generation to another, and mental imbalance is not God's will for our children. Neither is confused or unstable thinking.

A big part of having a sound mind has to do with what goes into it. Filling our minds with what is out in the world brings confusion. Filling our minds with the things of God—especially His Word—brings clarity of thought and peace of mind. The Bible says, "God is not the author of confusion but of peace" (1 Corinthians 14:33). We must do what we can to make sure our children have the Word of God in their minds so as to crowd out confusion and ensure they are soundminded.

God has *given* us a *sound mind.* Why should we accept anything less for our children? Ask God for it.

PRAYER

Lord,

Thank You for promising us a sound mind. I lay claim to that promise for (name of child). I pray that his (her) mind be clear, alert, bright, intelligent, stable, peaceful, and uncluttered. I pray there will be no confusion, no dullness, and no unbalanced, scattered, unorganized, or negative thinking. I pray that his (her) mind will not be filled with complex or confusing thoughts. Rather, give him (her) clarity of mind so that he (she) is able to think straight at all times. Give him (her) the ability to make clear decisions, to understand all he (she) needs to know, and to be able to focus on what he (she) needs to do. Where there is now any mental instability, impairment, or dysfunction, I speak healing in Jesus' name. May he (she) be renewed in the spirit of his (her) mind (Ephesians 4:23) and have the mind of Christ (1 Corinthians 2:16).

I pray that he (she) will so love the Lord with all his (her) heart, soul, and mind that there will be no room in him (her) for the lies of the Enemy

or the clamoring of the world. May the Word of
God take root in his (her) heart and fill his (her)
mind with things that are true, noble, just, pure,
lovely, of good report, virtuous, and praiseworthy
(Philippians 4:8). Give him (her) understanding
that what goes into his (her) mind becomes part
of him (her), so that he (she) will weigh carefully
what he (she) sees and hears.

You have said, "You will keep him in perfect
peace, whose mind is stayed on You, because he
trusts in You" (Isaiah 26:3). I pray that his (her)
faith in You and Your Word will grow daily so that
he (she) will live forever in peace and soundness
of mind.

WEAPONS OF WARFARE

Do not be conformed to this world, but be
transformed by the renewing of your mind, that
you may prove what is the good and acceptable
and perfect will of God.
ROMANS 12:2

Be anxious for nothing, but in everything by prayer
and supplication, with thanksgiving, let your requests
be made known to God; and the peace of God, which
surpasses all understanding, will guard your hearts
and minds through Christ Jesus.
PHILIPPIANS 4:6–7

For the weapons of our warfare are not carnal but
mighty in God for pulling down strongholds, casting
down arguments and every high thing that exalts itself
against the knowledge of God, bringing every thought
into captivity to the obedience of Christ.
2 CORINTHIANS 10:4–5

For to be carnally minded is death, but to be
spiritually minded is life and peace.
ROMANS 8:6

This I say, therefore, and testify in the Lord, that you
should no longer walk as the rest of the Gentiles walk,
in the futility of their mind, having their understanding
darkened, being alienated from the life of God,
because of the ignorance that is in them, because
of the blindness of their heart.
EPHESIANS 4:17–18

CHAPTER TWENTY-ONE

Inviting the Joy of the Lord

A young teenage girl came to me with very sad eyes, a furrowed brow, and a pinched and strained face. In the hour that followed she shared with me the pain of her life, crying as she talked. She was feeling nearly every negative emotion imaginable, including suicidal thoughts. I prayed with her about each matter of concern and then I asked God to give her "beauty for ashes, the oil of joy for mourning, the garment of praise for the spirit of heaviness" (Isaiah 61:3).

When we were done, I was amazed at the difference in her face. The joyless and tortured expression had been replaced by a radiant and calm beauty. A spirit of joy had already begun to take root, and she looked like a different person. Since then I have seen this girl blossom into such confidence and beauty that she is attractive to everyone around her.

Sadly, many young people today suffer with depression. And the worst part is that they carry it with them into adulthood. It comes and goes, putting a pall over their lives, affecting their work, upsetting their relationships, ruining their health, and even affecting how they view God.

This doesn't have to happen. No matter what kind of experiences a person has had, there is no need to live with depression or any other negative emotion. Don't allow your child to be stuck with a sad, depressed, angry, moody, or difficult personality. Pray them out of it.

It's easy to tell which people carry negative emotions inside and which ones have a spirit of joy. It's especially obvious in children, because they don't have the ability to hide their emotions the way we learn to do as adults.

Take a long look at your child. Is the common expression on his or her face one of peace, happiness, and joy? Or is it distress, frustration, dissatisfaction, anger, depression, or sadness? Does your child ever have a bad attitude for what seems to be no reason at all? Does your child ever seem down or moody and yet can't explain why? Take charge of that situation before it becomes a habit. Negative emotions are habit-forming if we don't put a stop to them by praying for our children to be overtaken by a spirit of joy.

Don't think for a moment that by praying for the joy of the Lord to fill your child you are creating a shallow person without compassion for the sufferings of others. This will never happen. The joy of the Lord is rich and deep and causes anyone who walks in it to be likewise. That's because joy doesn't have anything to do with happy circumstances; it has to do with looking into the face of God and knowing He's all we'll ever need.

I'm not saying that your child should never have a negative emotion or show emotional pain. I'm saying that negative emotions should not be a way of life. I'm saying that we should look to the Lord because "He brought forth His people with joy" (Psalm 105:43). He will bring forth our children in like manner if we ask it of Him.

PRAYER

Lord,

I pray that (name of child) be given the gift of joy. Let the spirit of joy rise up in her (his) heart this day and may she (he) know the fullness of joy that is found only in Your presence. Help her (him) to understand that true happiness and joy are found only in You.

Whenever she (he) is overtaken by negative emotions, surround her (him) with Your love. Teach her (him) to say, "This is the day that the Lord has made, we will rejoice and be glad in it" (Psalm 118:24). Deliver her (him) from despair, depression, loneliness, discouragement, anger, or rejection. May these negative attitudes have no place in (name of child), nor be a lasting part of her (his) life. May she (he) decide in her (his) heart, "My soul shall be joyful in the Lord; it shall rejoice in His salvation" (Psalm 35:9).

I know, Lord, that any negative emotions this child feels are lies, contrary to the truth of Your Word. Plant Your Word firmly in her (his) heart and increase her (his) faith daily. Enable her (him) to abide in Your love and derive strength from the joy of the Lord this day and forever.

WEAPONS OF WARFARE

If you keep My commandments, you will abide in My love, just as I have kept My Father's commandments and abide in His love. These things I have spoken to you, that My joy may remain in you, and that your joy may be full.
JOHN 15:10–11

You will show me the path of life; in Your presence is fullness of joy; at Your right hand are pleasures forevermore.
PSALM 16:11

Now may the God of hope fill you with all joy and peace in believing, that you may abound in hope by the power of the Holy Spirit.
ROMANS 15:13

His anger is but for a moment, His favor is for life; weeping may endure for a night, but joy comes in the morning.
PSALM 30:5

I will greatly rejoice in the Lord, my soul shall be joyful in my God; for He has clothed me with the garments of salvation, He has covered me with the robe of righteousness, as a bridegroom decks himself with ornaments, and as a bride adorns herself with her jewels.

ISAIAH **61:10**

CHAPTER TWENTY-TWO

Destroying an Inheritance of Family Bondage

We all know we can inherit our mother's eyes, our father's nose, or the color of our grandmother's hair. But did you know that we can also inherit a bad temper, a propensity for lying, depression, self-pity, envy, unforgiveness, perfectionism, and pride? These and other entrenched characteristics that have a spiritual base can also be passed along from our parents to us, and from us to our children. In a particular family there may be a tendency toward such things as divorce, constant sickness, infidelity, alcoholism, addiction, suicide, depression, rejection, or being accident prone—all mistakenly accepted as "fate" or "the way I am."

"These things just happen to my family," we hear people say.

Some of what we accept about ourselves and our lives are actually family bondages, for children can inherit the consequences of their ancestors' sins. The Bible says God will visit "the iniquities of the fathers upon the children to the third and fourth generations of those who hate Me" (Exodus 20:5). This Scripture is referring to people who don't walk in a loving relationship with God, but how many of our ancestors didn't walk with God and how many times have we been less than lovingly obedient to Him? The point is, we all qualify for the judgment in this verse, but by the grace of God, through Jesus Christ, we don't have to endure it. The very next verse continues by saying that God shows mercy "to those who love Me and keep My commandments" (Exodus 20:6).

Unlike physical traits, spiritual tendencies are something we don't have to receive. That's because they are usually nothing more than the unquestioned acceptance of a firmly entrenched lie of the Enemy. We can choose to break away from them through prayer and the power of the Holy Spirit.

When we see things we don't like about ourselves reflected in our children, we can do something about it. And if we've observed these same traits in our parents and grandparents, we can be *especially* diligent to pray specifically about breaking this generational bondage. For example, in some families where divorce is a repeated pattern, a child will grow up believing the lie that divorce is the way out when things get tough in a marriage relationship. But the lies of a spirit of divorce can be rendered powerless when exposed to the power of God and the truth of His Word.

"If God, through His mercy has saved us, and the Holy Spirit has washed and renewed us, and we are justified by grace, then why am I still struggling with sin?" I asked my Christian counselor a number of years ago.

"It's because the sin is either unconfessed, or you are choosing to continue to do it," he answered.

"I'm embarrassed to bring this up again," I said, "but I still have unforgiveness for various family members for things that have happened in the past. Why can't I get beyond this?"

"Your mother was an unforgiving person wasn't she?" he said.

"Very much so. She had unforgiveness for nearly every family member. That's why she distanced herself from most of them. She had few friends for the same reason—she pushed them away with her unforgiveness for the most minor infractions."

"Have you ever thought of the possibility that you could have inherited that tendency toward unforgiveness in your personality? Children pick up what their parents are," he suggested.

I'd never thought about the possibility of there being anything outside my own mind that was propelling me to stay locked in unforgiveness, but the more I thought about it, the more I remembered seeing that trait manifest seriously in other family members. Surely every family has that to deal with at some point, but most get beyond it without allowing a disagreement, riff, or infraction to cause a major breach in the family ties.

"I know this doesn't relieve me of my responsibility to forgive, but I do see a pattern of this in my family," I said. "And what frightens me most is that it could happen in my own children. I see them now hanging on to unforgiveness toward one another for things that have happened. It would break my heart to think that after they've grown and left our house, or after my husband and I have gone to be with the Lord, they would have nothing to do with one another. I can see that I have to get free of this for them as well as for myself."

The counselor and I prayed that day that the sin of unforgiveness in my family would not be passed down from generation to generation, but would be stopped by the power of the Holy Spirit. I proclaimed the truth of God's Word which says I am a new creation in Christ and I don't have to live according to the habits and sins of the past.

Through that revelation, I resolved to confess unforgiveness the moment it appeared—even if that meant doing it on an hour by hour basis. I prayed, and still pray, for God to make me a forgiving person. It's the easiest thing in the world to find something to be unforgiving about. It takes a stronger person to be willing to overlook a matter and focus on the Lord.

The more I have released unforgiveness through confession, repentance, and prayer before God, the more I have seen my children become free of it too. And their relationship with one another has become better. Of course, my children's ability to forgive does not rely on me. It is their decision. But hopefully they will see forgiveness being modeled in a clear enough manner as to make their decision to forgive easier.

A good way to see family bondage *broken* in your child is to see it broken in you first. The best place to start is to identify any sin in your life. Wherever there is sin, there is a spirit behind it. If that sin is given place time and again, the spirit behind it becomes more and more entrenched. For example, a lie is a sin and is accompanied by a lying spirit. By repeated lying, place is given to a lying spirit and soon lying gets out of control. Another example is wanting to die. This is a sin and behind it is a suicidal spirit. When someone says "I want to die" enough times, a spirit of suicide takes hold of their mind, and soon they are plagued by suicidal thoughts. If you see a place in your life where you have sinned or not lived God's way, repent of it immediately by going before the Lord and confessing it. Ask for God's forgiveness and say, "God, *You* be in control and help me not to live like that any more."

The next thing to do is identify any bondage in your parents or grandparents that you feel could be affecting you or your children and pray about that also. The Bible says, "For you did not receive the spirit of bondage again to fear, but you received the Spirit of adoption by whom we cry out, 'Abba, Father.' The Spirit Himself bears witness with our spirit that we are children of God, and if children, then heirs—heirs of God and joint heirs with Christ" (Romans 8:15–17). We want to be heirs of God, not of our family's sin.

In Jesus' name we can be set free from any family bondage, and by the power of the Holy Spirit we can refuse to allow it any place in our children's lives. If you can think of any family traits you don't want your children to inherit, start praying now.

PRAYER

Lord,

You have said in Your Word that a good man leaves an inheritance to his children's children (Proverbs 13:22). I pray that the inheritance I leave to my children will be the rewards of a godly life and a clean heart before You. To make sure that happens, I ask that wherever there is any kind of bondage in me that I have inherited from my family and accepted as mine, deliver me from it now in the name of Jesus. I confess the sins of my family to You. I don't even know what all of them are, but I know that You do. I ask for forgiveness and restoration. I also confess my own sins to You and ask for forgiveness, knowing Your Word says, "If we confess our sins, He is faithful and just to forgive us our sins and cleanse us from all unrighteousness" (1 John 1:9). I know that cleansing from sin through confession eliminates the possibility of passing the consequences of sin on to my child.

Jesus said, "I give you the authority . . . over all the powers of the enemy" (Luke 10:19). If there is any work of the Enemy in my family's past that seeks to encroach upon the life of my child, (name of child), I break it now by the power and authority given me in Jesus Christ. I pray specifically about (name something you see in yourself or your family that you don't want passed on to your child). Whatever is not Your will for our lives, I reject as sin.

Thank You, Jesus, that You came to set us free from the past. We refuse to live bound by it. Thank You, Father, that You have "qualified us to be partakers of the inheritance of the saints in the light" (Colossians 1:12). I pray that my son (daughter) will not inherit any bondage from his (her) earthly family, but will "inherit the kingdom prepared for him (her) from the foundation of the world" (Matthew 25:34). Thank You, Jesus, that in You the old has passed away and all things are new.

WEAPONS OF WARFARE

Stand fast therefore in the liberty by which Christ
has made us free, and do not be entangled
again with a yoke of bondage.
GALATIANS 5:1

Blessed be the God and Father of our Lord Jesus
Christ, who according to His abundant mercy
has begotten us again to a living hope through the

resurrection of Jesus Christ from the dead, to an inheritance incorruptible and undefiled and that does not fade away, reserved in heaven for you, who are kept by the power of God through faith for salvation ready to be revealed in the last time.

1 PETER 1:3–5

The Spirit of the Lord God is upon Me, because the Lord has anointed Me to preach good tidings to the poor; He has sent Me to heal the brokenhearted, to proclaim liberty to the captives, and the opening of the prison to those who are bound.

ISAIAH 61:1

Therefore, if anyone is in Christ, he is a new creation; old things have passed away; behold, all things have become new.

2 CORINTHIANS 5:17

For we ourselves were also once foolish, disobedient, deceived, serving various lusts and pleasures, living in malice and envy, hateful and hating one another. But when the kindness and the love of God our Savior toward man appeared, not by works of righteousness which we have done, but according to His mercy He saved us, through the washing of regeneration and renewing of the Holy Spirit, whom He poured out on us abundantly through Jesus Christ our Savior, that having been justified by His grace we should become heirs according to the hope of eternal life.

TITUS 3:3–7

CHAPTER TWENTY-THREE

Avoiding Alcohol, Drugs, and Other Addictions

Satan wants our children, and he'll take them any way he can. Alcohol, drugs, and other addictions are some of his most successful lures. In fact, the attack against our children is so great that they cannot stand against it without our support. The good news is that *with* our support, prayer covering, and teaching, they can stand firm.

It's never too soon to start praying for our children to avoid alcohol and drugs, because the exposure to and possibility of addiction to these substances can happen at a very early age. It's also never too late to pray about it either, because temptation can happen to anyone at any point in their lives. I know someone who didn't become an alcoholic until he was in his fifties. He said he knew he had a weakness for it, but didn't give in to it until he was at a small dinner party where liquor was being served. He tried a little, and when he went home he didn't stop drinking. Perhaps if he'd had a praying parent or a prayer group interceding for him this would never have happened.

I've seen many Christian music ministries go under because of alcohol and drugs. These people are out on the front lines of battle and don't even realize it until they are shot down. They are prime targets for Enemy attack, and they fall right into his traps because they are not covered in prayer. Granted, some of them willfully give in to temptation, but I believe that most of them want to do what's right. The point is, the draw of the flesh and the Devil's plans are a lot stronger than we'd like to think. In a moment of weakness, such as is possible for all of us, we can end up doing something we never thought we would. Only the power of God, through prayer, can make the difference.

If your child *already* has a problem in this area and the Devil has won some ground in the battle, stand up in the confidence of knowing who you are in the Lord and gain it back. Your children are *yours* and *not* the Devil's, and you can make a case for them before the throne of God. *You* have the power *and* the authority. Satan doesn't. All he has to work with are lies and deception. Rebuke his lies by the power invested in you through Jesus Christ your Savior, who is Lord over everything in your life, including your child.

The Bible says, "Therefore, whether you eat or drink, or whatever you do, do all to the glory of God"

(1 Corinthians 10:31). Let's pray that everything our children do with their bodies be done to God's glory.

PRAYER

Lord,

    I pray that You would keep (name of child) free from any addiction—especially to alcohol or drugs. Make her (him) strong in You, draw her (him) close and enable her (him) to put You in control of her (his) life. Speak to her (his) heart, show her (him) the path she (he) should walk, and help her (him) see that protecting her (his) body from things that destroy it is a part of her (his) service to You.

    I pray that You, Lord, would thwart any plan Satan has to destroy her (his) life through alcohol and drugs, and take away anything in her (his) personality that would be drawn to those substances. Your Word says, "There is a way that seems right to a man, but its end is the way of death" (Proverbs 16:25). Give her (him) discernment and strength to be able to say "no" to things that bring death and "yes" to the things of God that bring life. May she (he) clearly see the truth whenever tempted and be delivered from the Evil One whenever trapped. Enable her (him) to choose life in whatever she (he) does, and may her (his) only addiction be to the things of God.

In Jesus' name I pray that everything she (he) does with her (his) body be done to Your glory.

WEAPONS OF WARFARE

If you live according to the flesh you will die;
but if by the Spirit you put to death the
deeds of the body, you will live.
ROMANS 8:13

Therefore remove sorrow from your heart,
and put away evil from your flesh.
ECCLESIASTES 11:10

I have set before you life and death, blessing
and cursing; therefore choose life, that both
you and your descendants may live.
DEUTERONOMY 30:19

The righteousness of the upright will deliver them, but
the unfaithful will be caught by their lust.
PROVERBS 11:6

Therefore if the Son makes you free,
you shall be free indeed.
JOHN 8:36

CHAPTER TWENTY-FOUR

Rejecting Sexual Immorality

Next to catastrophic injury, death, and eternal hell, sexual immorality is the most dreaded possibility for our children's lives. That's because the results of sexual sin last a lifetime—often for the parents as well as the child. Words like "abortion," "out-of-wedlock," "infidelity," "homosexuality," "sexually transmitted disease," and "AIDS" all make a parent shudder. And today, more than ever before, this is a life and death issue.

We are all well aware that there is no way out of sexual immorality without consequences. But it's not only what happens to our children's bodies that concerns us. The Bible says, "Abstain from fleshly lusts which war against the soul" (1 Peter 2:11). The consequences of sexual sin invade the soul as well.

This is something I've prayed about from the time my children were little, and I pray as fervently today. I certainly don't want them dying from AIDS, nor do I want grandchildren before my children are married.

167

Aside from those major points, I also do not want them to disobey God and miss out on all He has for them. I know that with sexual sin the fullness of God's presence, peace, blessing, and joy is sacrificed. The price is way too high.

We can't wait until our children are teenagers to pray about this, just as we can't wait until then to instruct them that life works better when we live God's way. Today is the day to pray. Sexual temptation is everywhere. It's in front of our children's eyes at every turn. It's on billboards, TV, and radio; it's in movies, popular music, books, and magazines—even such innocuous publications as those having to do with news, sports, health, and hobbies. Our children are bombarded by it, and we are living in denial if we think they cannot be tempted. They can, and the force will be strong. They need us interceding on their behalf. Even if your child has already failed in this area, it is never too late for them to confess and repent, and be forgiven, healed, and made new.

The Bible says, "He who trusts in his own heart is a fool, but whoever walks wisely will be delivered" (Proverbs 28:26). We must pray for our children to trust God and not their unreliable emotions, so that they will walk with wisdom and avoid this dangerous trap. We must pray for them to live God's way.

One of God's ways for our lives is sexual purity, and the foundation for it is laid at a very young age. No matter what age your child is—a toddler, a teenager, or a thirty-something—and whether a virgin or sexually active—start praying for him or her to live a life of sexual purity from this day forward.

PRAYER

Lord,

I pray that You will keep (name of child) sexually pure all of his (her) life. Give him (her) a heart that wants to do what's right in this area, and let purity take root in his (her) personality and guide his (her) actions. Help him (her) to always lay down godly rules for relationships and resist anything that is not Your best. Open his (her) eyes to the truth of Your Word, and help him (her) to see that sex outside of marriage will never be the committed, lasting, unconditional love that he (she) needs. Let his (her) personality not be scarred nor his (her) emotions damaged by the fragmentation of the soul that happens as a result of sexual immorality.

I pray that he (she) will have no premarital sex and no sex with anyone other than his (her) marriage partner. I pray that homosexuality will never take root in him (her) or even have an opportunity to express itself toward him (her). Keep him (her) away from the presence of anyone with evil intentions, or take that person out of his (her) life. Protect him (her) from any sexual molestation or rape. Turn his (her) eyes away from the sexual immorality that saturates the

world and enable him (her) to understand that
whoever "wants to be a friend of the world makes
himself an enemy of God" (James 4:4). May he
(she) long for *Your* approval, Lord, and not allow
sexual sin in his (her) life at any time. Deliver him
(her) from any spirit of lust bringing temptation to
fail in this area. Put a Holy Spirit alarm in him
(her) that goes off like a loud, flashing siren
whenever he (she) steps over the line of what is
right in Your sight.

Your Word says, "Blessed is the man who
endures temptation; for when he has been proved,
he will receive the crown of life which the Lord
has promised to those who love Him" (James
1:12). Speak loudly to him (her) whenever there
is temptation to do something he (she) shouldn't,
and make him (her) strong enough in You to
stand for what's right and say "No" to sexual
immorality. May Your grace enable him (her) to
be committed to staying pure so that he (she) will
receive Your crown of life.

WEAPONS OF WARFARE

This is the will of God, your sanctification: that you
should abstain from sexual immorality; that each of
you should know how to possess his own vessel in
sanctification and honor, not in passion of lust, like
the Gentiles who do not know God.

1 THESSALONIANS 4:3–5

Flee sexual immorality. Every sin that a man does
is outside the body, but he who commits sexual
immorality sins against his own body.
1 CORINTHIANS 6:18

The body is not for sexual immorality but for the Lord,
and the Lord for the body.
1 CORINTHIANS 6:13

No temptation has overtaken you except such as
is common to man; but God is faithful, He will not
allow you to be tempted beyond what you are able,
but with the temptation will also make the way of
escape, that you may be able to bear it.
1 CORINTHIANS 10:13

But each one is tempted when he is drawn away by
his own desires and enticed. Then, when desire
has conceived, it gives birth to sin; and sin, when
it is full-grown, brings forth death.
JAMES 1:14–15

CHAPTER TWENTY-FIVE

Finding the Perfect Mate

Shortly after my son and daughter were born, I started praying for their respective wife and husband. I'm still praying, and will be until they are married. Along with that, I pray that a spirit of divorce will never have any place in either of their lives. Some may think these prayers premature. They are not. Next to their decision to receive Jesus, marriage is the most important decision our children will ever make. It will affect the rest of their lives, not to mention the lives of other family members. The wrong decision can bring misery and pain for everyone concerned. And since only God knows who will make the best marriage partner for anyone, He should be consulted first and He should give the final answer.

When I think of the people I know who have experienced miserable marriages, abusive spouses, marital infidelity, multiple marriages, being married too late to have children, or who are unhappily single, one thing

173

stands out in my mind: none of them had parents who interceded on their behalf for their mate and their marriage relationship.

On the other hand, I know couples who are perfectly matched in the bond of marriage and who have suffered none of the aforementioned problems. Not surprisingly, all of these individuals had parents who prayed for them in this regard or the individuals themselves prayed and waited until they were certain they'd found the mate God had chosen for them. Also, these individuals did not flit from one affair to another or ignore God's rules for sexual purity. They kept themselves pure for the mate God had for them, and they have been greatly rewarded.

As a result of all these observations and my own experience, I now believe that marriages can literally be made in heaven when we pray to the ultimate matchmaker.

Magnificent weddings do not make perfect marriages. Only God can do that. The Bible says, "There are many plans in a man's heart, nevertheless the Lord's counsel—that will stand" (Proverbs 19:21). It's not bridal consultants and caterers who set the bride and groom on the right path. Consulting God and following His leading does that. And only prayer keeps our children continually seeking God's will instead of following their own emotions.

The Spirit of God keeps a marriage together; a spirit of divorce destroys it. Pray now that the Holy Spirit, not a spirit of divorce, will rule your child's future.

If your child is already married to someone, pray that he or she and his or her mate will "be perfectly joined together in the same mind" (1 Corinthians 1:10), because every "house divided against itself will not stand" (Matthew 12:25). Pray that they will be delivered from any spirit of divorce that would try to drive a wedge between them. If your child is already divorced, pray for all brokenness to be healed and that there will be no more divorce in his or her future.

No matter what age your child is, pray about this today. Divorce is a part of the spirit of this age, and it threatens everyone at one time or another. Let's stand together to resist it for ourselves and our children by the power of the Holy Spirit in us through Jesus Christ, God's Son.

PRAYER

Lord,

I pray that unless Your plan is for her (him) to remain single, You will send the perfect marriage partner for (name of child). Send the right husband (wife) at the perfect time, and give her (him) a clear leading from You as to who it is. I pray that my daughter (son) will be submissive enough to hear Your voice when it comes time to make a marriage decision, and that she (he) will make that decision based on what *You* are saying and not just fleshly desire. I pray that she (he) will trust You with all her (his) heart and lean not on her (his) own understanding; that she (he) will acknowledge You in all her (his) ways so that You will direct her (his) path (Proverbs 3:5–6).

Prepare that person who will make the perfect husband (wife) for her (him). Help my daughter (my son) to know the difference between simply falling in love and knowing for certain this is the person with whom God wants her (him) to spend the rest of her (his) life. If she (he) becomes attracted to someone she (he) shouldn't marry, I pray that You, Lord, would cut off the relationship. Help her (him) to realize that unless You are at the center of the marriage, it will never stand. Unless You bless it, it won't be blessed. For Your Word says, "Unless the Lord builds the house, they labor in vain who build it" (Psalm 127:1). I pray that You would build the marriage around which their house is established.

When she (he) does find the right one to marry, I pray that person will be a godly and devoted servant of Yours, who loves You and lives Your way, and will be like a son (daughter) to me and a blessing to all other family members. Once she (he) is married, let there be no divorce in her (his) future. May there never be mental, emotional, or physical abuse of any kind, but rather mental, emotional, and physical unity that is never touched by division. I pray for their deliverance from any spirit of divorce, separation, or disunity that would attempt to drive a wedge into their relationship. Give them each a strong desire to live in fidelity, and remove any temptation to infidelity.

May she (he) have one mate for life, who is also her (his) closest friend. May they be mutually loyal, compassionate, considerate, sensitive, respectful, affectionate, forgiving, supportive, caring, and loving toward one another all the days of their lives.

WEAPONS OF WARFARE

From the beginning of the creation, God made them male and female. For this reason a man shall leave his father and mother and be joined to his wife, and the two shall become one flesh; so then they are no longer two, but one flesh. Therefore what God has joined together, let not man separate.

MARK 10:6–9

Marriage is honorable among all, and the bed undefiled; but fornicators and adulterers God will judge.

HEBREWS 13:4

Whoever divorces his wife and marries another commits adultery against her.

MARK 10:11

He who finds a wife finds a good thing, and obtains favor from the Lord.

PROVERBS 18:22

You cover the altar of the LORD with tears, with weeping
and crying; so He does not regard the offering anymore, nor receive it with good will from your hands.
Yet you say, "For what reason?" Because the LORD has
been witness between you and the wife of your youth,
with whom you have dealt treacherously; yet she is
your companion and your wife by covenant. But did
He not make them one, having a remnant of the Spirit?
And why one? He seeks godly offspring. Therefore
take heed to your spirit, and let none deal treacherously with the wife of his youth. For the LORD God of
Israel says that He hates divorce.

MALACHI 2:13–16

CHAPTER TWENTY-SIX

Living Free of Unforgiveness

Whenever I have to apologize to my children for something, I tell them I need to hear them say, "I forgive you." I don't do that just because *I* need to *hear* it; I do it because *they* need to *say* it and be completely released. Likewise, if my children argue with each other, I ask them to say "I'm sorry" and "I forgive you" to one another. Even if they don't wholeheartedly feel those things at the time, I know that what they say will eventually work its way into their soul. Of course it's best if they say these things and mean them without ever having to be told, but until that becomes a reality, this is far better than doing nothing and just waiting for forgiveness to happen.

"Forgiveness is a *choice* you make," I've instructed them. "If you don't forgive, it brings death into your life in one form or another. The best way to become forgiving is to pray for the person you need to forgive. Even though it may seem hard at first, once you get into it

179

and find more and more things to pray about, you'll notice your heart becoming soft toward that person."

I've observed firsthand, as I'm sure you have, families who wait for forgiveness to happen. They don't forgive until they *feel like* forgiving. As a result, there are often serious rifts among family members. They habitually say unkind things *to* or *about* one another, or perhaps haven't even spoken in years. A distinct lack of graciousness and mutual appreciation undergirds every word and deed because a spirit of unforgiveness has been given a home there. A whole family suffers when one or more of its members walk in an unforgiving stance toward one another.

As a part of honoring father and mother and receiving the promise of long life and blessing that accompanies that commandment, every child needs to forgive both parents for their imperfections and anything they may have done that was hurtful. Along with that they also need to forgive sisters, brothers, aunts, uncles, cousins, grandparents, acquaintances, friends, enemies, and sometimes even themselves—and we need to encourage them to do it. If we don't teach our children to forgive, we're doing them a disservice that may have serious consequences.

One of the best things we can do to help our children stay free of unforgiveness, besides teaching *them* to be forgiving and praying that they walk in forgiveness, is to get free of unforgiveness ourselves. Unforgiveness can so easily become a part of our lives that we take it along with us wherever we go without even realizing we are carrying this excess baggage.

When I finally learned that forgiveness doesn't make the *other person right,* it makes *you free,* I found great breakthrough in that area. I always felt that forgiving someone meant I was saying, "What you did is okay." But that's not the case at all. Forgiveness is trusting that God is the God of justice He says He is and saying, "Father, I won't hold that person to myself with unforgiveness anymore." It's acknowledging that God knows the truth and allowing Him to be the judge, because He is the only one who knows the whole story.

The Bible says, "The Lord is a God of justice; blessed are all those who wait for Him" (Isaiah 30:18). We will be blessed if we confess our unforgiveness to Him, pray to be delivered from it, and then sit back and wait for God to do the right thing while we enjoy His blessings. Doesn't that sound a lot more enjoyable than living in the prison of unforgiveness and suffering the disease it brings into our souls, bodies, relationships, and lives?

How does the son forgive the father who beat him? How does the mother forgive the drunk driver who killed her daughter? How does the young girl forgive the uncle who molested her? How can anyone show mercy for someone who was merciless? They can't fully, unless they come into the presence of the Lord and understand His *complete* forgiveness. There is nothing like the tears of joy and release we feel when we come to that place of complete forgiveness before the Lord. It's life-giving because it renews our entire being. The Bible says, "One thing I do, forgetting those things which are behind and reaching forward to those things which are ahead, I press toward the goal for the prize of the upward call of God in Christ Jesus" (Philippians 3:13–14).

We cannot get on with our lives and all that God has for us as long as we are bound and tethered to the past. Neither can our children. Jesus said, "Blessed are the merciful, for they shall obtain mercy" (Matthew 5:7). Let's pray for our children to show mercy so nothing will limit God's mercy toward them. Let's pray for them to be people who say "I forgive you" whenever the opportunity presents itself.

Let's pray that bitterness and unforgiveness do not become a wall between us and God and hinder our prayers. We don't have time for that. There is too much praying to be done.

PRAYER

Lord,
I pray that You would enable (name of child) to live in ongoing forgiveness. Teach him (her) the depth of Your forgiveness toward him (her) so that he (she) can be freely forgiving toward others. Help him (her) to make the decision to forgive based on what You've asked us to do and not on what feels good at the moment. May he (she) understand that forgiveness doesn't justify the other person's

actions; instead, it makes him (her) *free.* Help him (her) to understand that only You know the whole story about any of us, and that's why he (she) doesn't have the right to judge.

Lord, Your Word says, "He who loves his brother abides in the light, and there is no cause for stumbling in him. But he who hates his brother is in darkness and walks in darkness, and does not know where he is going, because the darkness has blinded his eyes" (1 John 2:10–11). Show me places where I walk in the darkness of unforgiveness. I don't want that in my life. I want to see clearly and know where I'm going. And I pray that for my child as well. May he (she) always walk in the light of love and forgiveness. Enable him (her) to forgive family members, friends, and all others as well. Teach him (her) to release the past to You so that he (she) can move into all that You have for him (her). Don't allow him (her) to harbor resentment, bitterness, and anger, but rather help him (her) to turn these feelings over to you immediately whenever they creep in.

I pray that he (she) will forgive himself (herself) for times of failure, and may he (she) never blame You, Lord, for things that happen on this earth and in his (her) life. According to Your Word I pray that he (she) will love his (her) enemies, bless those who curse him (her), do good to those who hate him (her), and pray for those who spitefully use and persecute him (her), so that he (she) may enjoy all Your blessings (Matthew 5:44–45). In Jesus' name, I pray that he (she) will live in the fullness of Your forgiveness for him (her) and walk in the freedom of forgiveness in his (her) own heart.

WEAPONS OF WARFARE

Let all bitterness, wrath, anger, clamor, and evil speaking be put away from you, with all malice. And be kind to one another, tenderhearted, forgiving one another, just as God in Christ also forgave you.
EPHESIANS 4:31–32

If you forgive men their trespasses, your heavenly Father will also forgive you. But if you do not forgive men their trespasses, neither will your Father forgive your trespasses.
MATTHEW 6:14–15

His master was angry, and delivered him to the torturers until he should pay all that was due to him. So My heavenly Father also will do to you if each of you, from his heart, does not forgive his brother his trespasses.
MATTHEW 18:34–35

The discretion of a man makes him slow to anger, and it is to his glory to overlook a transgression.
PROVERBS 19:11

Whenever you stand praying, if you have anything against anyone, forgive him, that your Father in heaven may also forgive you your trespasses.
MARK 11:25

CHAPTER TWENTY-SEVEN

Walking in Repentance

Have you ever noticed children who live in guilt and condemnation because they have not been disciplined to confess, repent, and be forgiven of their sins? They don't have the same clear-eyed, confident faces that children who are free of condemnation have. The Bible says, "They looked to Him and were radiant and their faces were not ashamed" (Psalm 34:5). Children who admit their mistakes and are sorry enough about them to want to change their ways have an entirely different countenance than those who hide their sin and have no intention of being different.

Confession and repentance are two life principles we must insist upon for our children, because unconfessed sin will put a wall between them and God. Repentance, which literally means "turning away and deciding not to do it again," is manifested when the child says, in effect, "I did this, I'm sorry about it, and I'm not going to do it again." If sin is not confessed and repented of in that way, the child can't be free of the bondage that goes along with unconfessed sin, and that will show on his (her) face and in his (her) personality and actions.

God said to the Israelites who disobeyed Him and didn't repent of it, "You shall remember your ways and all your doings with which you were defiled; and you shall loathe yourselves in your own sight because of all the evils that you have committed" (Ezekiel 20:43). That self-loathing for unconfessed and unrepented sin is *our* lot as well, and one of its manifestations is a poor self-image. Such feelings of failure and guilt will wreak destruction in our children's lives if they are not taught to confess and repent.

I remember detecting sin on my children's faces before I ever discovered it in their actions. They used to tell me how irritating it was that they could never get away with anything for long.

"That's because I asked God to reveal to me anything I need to know," I told them, "and the Holy Spirit always tells me if you've done something wrong."

Whenever I saw their open, clear-eyed countenances clouded by a dishonest demeanor, I would ask God to show me any hidden sin. After they had confessed and repented and received the appropriate punishment, their faces looked totally different—as though a weight or a shadow had been lifted from them. Sin has a toxic effect. Unconfessed sin weighs us down; it distorts and darkens our image. Confessed sin and a repentant heart bring light, life, confidence, and freedom.

Because no child is perfect, we need to ask God to reveal, expose, or bring to light any hidden sin that has taken root in our children's hearts so it can be dealt with now rather than later when the consequences are far more serious. God will do that, "for He knows the secrets of the heart (Psalm 44:21). We've all heard stories of the "nice, likeable man" who beats his wife, abuses his children, or goes on a killing spree. You can be sure that he was a man who had hidden sin in his heart. We can be just as sure that any hidden sin in our children will eventually display itself in an undesirable way. The time to catch it is now. "Cast away from you all the transgressions which you have committed, and get yourselves a new heart and a new spirit. For why should you die?" (Ezekiel 18:31). Ask God to bring any hidden sin in you or your children to light so there won't be a physical and emotional price to pay for it.

Sin leads to death. Repentance leads to life. We don't confess so that God will find out something. He already knows. Confession is a chance for us to clear the slate. Repentance is an opportunity for us to start over. Our children, as do we, need both.

PRAYER

Lord,

I pray that You would give (name of child) a heart that is quick to confess her (his) mistakes. May she (he) be truly repentant of them so that she (he) can be forgiven and cleansed. Help her (him) to understand that Your laws are for her (his) benefit and that the confession and repentance You require must become a way of life. Give her (him) the desire to live in truth before You, and may she (he) say as David did, "Wash me thoroughly from my iniquity, and cleanse me from my sin. Create in me a clean heart, O God, and renew a steadfast spirit within me. Do not cast me away from Your presence, and do not take Your Holy Spirit from me. Restore to me the joy of Your salvation" (Psalm 51:2,10–12).

Lord, bring to light any hidden sins so they can be confessed, repented of, and forgiven. Your Word says, "Blessed is he whose transgression is forgiven, whose sin is covered" (Psalm 32:1). I pray that my daughter (son) will never be able to contain sin within her (him), but rather let there be a longing to confess fully and say, "See if there is any wicked way in me, and lead me in the way everlasting" (Psalm 139:24). May she (he) not live in guilt and condemnation, but rather dwell with a clear conscience in the full understanding of her (his) forgiveness in Christ. I pray that she (he) will always look to You and wear a radiant countenance.

WEAPONS OF WARFARE

Beloved, if our heart does not condemn us, we have confidence toward God. And whatever we ask we

receive from Him, because we keep His commandments
and do those things that are pleasing in His sight.
1 JOHN 3:21–22

Let the wicked forsake his way, and the unrighteous
man his thoughts; let him return to the Lord, and
He will have mercy on him; and to our God, for
He will abundantly pardon.
ISAIAH 55:7

"Therefore I will judge you, O house of Israel, every
one according to his ways," says the Lord God.
"Repent, and turn from all your transgressions, so
that iniquity will not be your ruin."
EZEKIEL 18:30

He who covers his sins will not prosper, but whoever
confesses and forsakes them will have mercy.
PROVERBS 28:13

Repent therefore and be converted, that your sins may
be blotted out, so that times of refreshing may come
from the presence of the Lord.
ACTS 3:19

CHAPTER TWENTY-EIGHT

Breaking Down Ungodly Strongholds

Have you ever observed something in your child that bothers you but you can't identify what it is? When that happens, don't ignore your God-given instincts. Ask God to reveal what it is you're sensing. We are aligned with the Creator of the universe, who understands perfectly what is going on, and we need to ask Him for wisdom and revelation.

Have you ever detected an expression on your child's face that you knew was guilt but you didn't know the reason for it? In other words, you suspected an offense worthy of some kind of discipline but you didn't have the hard evidence. Whenever that happened with either of my children, I prayed, "Lord, You know our foolishness and our sins are not hidden from You (Psalm 69:5). Reveal to me what I am sensing in this child." Each time He revealed an ungodly stronghold erecting itself in the flesh. For instance, one time one of the children was smuggling forbidden foods into the bedroom for secret consumption. Another time, a lie was being set in motion in order to achieve a desired result. In every case the sins were revealed *after* I prayed.

I always told my children it wasn't worth it for them to disobey their mom and dad because God would always reveal it to us. They soon believed me.

One particular instance stands out in my mind. It occurred when Amanda was about seven years old. Every morning I gave her three tiny vitamins to swallow. These had been prescribed by our doctor, and I always made sure she had them in a tiny dish by her plate at the breakfast table. In the beginning she protested every time she had to take them. After awhile she became more cheerful about it, and eventually she stopped complaining altogether. Around the same time, I sensed something about Amanda that troubled me, but I couldn't put my finger on exactly what it was.

"Show me, Lord. Is there anything in Amanda I should be seeing?" I prayed.

Nothing happened over the next several days, and I didn't think much about it because I was busy packing our household goods for a move to another location. The day the moving company came to pack the large items, we started to remove the little cushions that were tied to the seats of the kitchen chairs. There, under Amanda's seat cushion, I found twenty-six little vitamins spread all around the seat. I couldn't believe my eyes. I called my husband in to show him what I'd found, and we both chuckled, even though we knew she'd have to be confronted when she arrived home from school.

We proceeded to untie the other five cushions and, much to our amazement, under all but one we discovered twenty to thirty vitamins. Only the chair furthest away from hers was empty. This time we rolled with laughter.

When Amanda arrived home from school, we wiped the smiles off our faces and presented her with well over a hundred vitamins and a cup of water. We told her that unless she wanted to take all those vitamins she had better do some explaining.

This incident seems humorous and minor, but if Amanda's deception had gone undetected and never dealt with, it could have led to bigger deceptions until deception had a foothold in her life. I'm grateful to God that He reveals such things to us *before* they become serious.

It doesn't necessarily have to be a child's sins you are sensing. It could be hurt or fear over something he (she) has thought, seen, or experienced. It could be hopelessness, confusion, envy, selfishness, or pride. It's impossible to guess, so it's best to ask God to reveal it to you. Even if you don't get a clear leading right away, you can still pray about it. Jesus instructed us to pray as a matter of course, "Deliver us from the evil one" (Matthew 6:13). Sometimes we don't have to be any more specific than praying for God to penetrate the lives of our children by the power of His Spirit and deliver them from evil. The point is, don't ignore these warnings.

Even if you don't sense anything in your child now, it's still a good preventative measure to pray the following prayer. Not that you have to be forever suspicious of your children, but you do have to be suspicious of the Enemy lurking around waiting to erect a stronghold in their lives. "Be sober, be vigilant; because your adversary the devil walks about like a roaring lion, seeking whom he may devour" (1 Peter 5:8). The verse following that one gives us directions on how to deal with this: *"Resist him,"* it says. Shall we pray?

PRAYER

Lord,
    Thank You that You have promised in Your Word to deliver us when we cry out to You. I come to You on behalf of (name of child) and ask that You would deliver him (her) from any ungodliness that may be threatening to become a stronghold in his (her) life. Even though I don't know what he (she) needs to be set free from, You do. I pray in the name of Jesus that You will work deliverance in his (her) life wherever it is needed. I know that although "we walk in the flesh, we do not war according to the flesh. For the weapons of our warfare are not carnal but mighty in God for pulling down strongholds, casting down arguments and every high thing that exalts itself against the knowledge of God" (2 Corinthians 10:3–5).

Give me wisdom and revelation regarding him (her). I know there are areas of Enemy operation which I cannot see, so I depend on You, Lord, to reveal these to me as I need to know them. Speak to my heart. Show me how to pray when there is something deep in my spirit that is unsettled, disturbed, or troubled about him (her). Show me anything that I am not seeing, and let all that is hidden come to light. If there is any action I need to take, I depend on You to show me. Thank You that You help me parent this child.

Lord, I put (name of child) in Your hands this day. Guide, protect, and convict him (her) when sin is trying to take root. Strengthen him (her) in battle when Satan attempts to gain a foothold in his (her) heart. Make him (her) sensitive to Enemy encroachment, and may he (she) run to You to be his (her) stronghold and refuge in times of trouble. May the cry of his (her) heart be, "Cleanse me from secret faults" (Psalm 19:12). According to Your Word I say that the Lord will deliver him (her) from every evil work and preserve him (her) for His heavenly kingdom (2 Timothy 4:18).

WEAPONS OF WARFARE

I will give you the keys of the kingdom of heaven,
and whatever you bind on earth will be bound
in heaven, and whatever you loose on earth
will be loosed in heaven.
MATTHEW 16:19

There is nothing covered that will not be revealed,
and hidden that will not be known.
MATTHEW 10:26

Though they join forces, the wicked will not
go unpunished; but the posterity of the
righteous will be delivered.
PROVERBS 11:21

The Lord also will be a refuge for the oppressed,
a refuge in times of trouble.
PSALM 9:9

Call to Me, and I will answer you, and show you great
and mighty things, which you do not know.
JEREMIAH 33:3

CHAPTER TWENTY-NINE

Seeking Wisdom and Discernment

Will my child know not to get into a car with a stranger? Will she see that playing near deep water is dangerous? Will he just say "No" when peers offer him drugs? Will she remember to look both ways before crossing a street? Will he ask the wrong girl to marry him? Will they be able to sense danger when it is imminent? So much of our children's safety and well-being depends on decisions they alone will make. The possible outcome of those decisions can seem frightening to a parent.

We can't ever be sure they'll make the right decision unless they have the gifts of wisdom, revelation, and discernment, along with an ear tuned to God's voice. The only way to secure any of those things is to seek God for them. The Bible says, "If any of you lacks wisdom, let him ask of God, who gives to all liberally and without reproach, and it will be given to him" (James 1:5).

Have you ever had times in your life when you knew God's wisdom was in control and you made the right decision in spite of yourself? Perhaps you decided not to complete a left turn, even though the light was with you; and sure enough, an oncoming car ran the light. You did the right thing, but you can't take the credit. Some people may view that as a coincidence. I believe it is the wisdom and discernment of God. And more times than we even know, it saves our lives.

We want that same wisdom and discernment flowing in our children's lives, for as they grow older they make more and more important decisions without us. Certain decisions my son had to make after graduating from high school caused me to sit on the sidelines holding my breath and praying, "Give him wisdom, Lord. Let him have a clear leading from You." God answered those prayers, and we see now how right Christopher's decisions were—for reasons only God could have known.

The old proverb that says, "A wise son makes a glad father, but a foolish son is the grief of his mother" (Proverbs 10:1), is completely accurate. No one can be prouder than Dad when his child makes a wise decision. But when a child acts without wisdom, no one grieves more deeply than a mother. Proverbs also says if we cry out for discernment and seek it like a hidden treasure we will find all the knowledge of God (Proverbs 2:3-5). I believe that's all the knowledge, wisdom, and discernment we could possibly need. Let's cry out to God and save ourselves some grief, shall we?

PRAYER

Lord,

I pray that You would give the gifts of wisdom, discernment, and revelation to (name of child). Help her (him) to trust You with all her (his) heart, not depending on her (his) own understanding, but acknowledging You in all her (his) ways so that she (he) may hear Your clear direction as to which path to take (Proverbs 3:5). Help her (him) to discern good from evil and be sensitive to the voice of the Holy Spirit saying, "This is the way, walk in it" (Isaiah 30:21). I know that much of her (his) happiness in life depends on gaining wisdom and discernment, which Your Word says brings long life, wealth, recognition, protection, enjoy-ment, contentment, and happiness. I want all those things for her (him), but I want them to come as blessings from You.

Your Word says, "The fear of the Lord is the beginning of wisdom, and the knowledge of the Holy One is understanding" (Proverbs 9:10). May a healthy fear and knowledge of You be the foundation upon which wisdom and discernment are established in her (him). May she (he) turn to You for all decisions so that she (he) doesn't make poor choices. Help her (him) to see that all the treasures of wisdom and knowledge are hidden in You and that You give of them freely when we ask for them. As she (he) seeks wisdom and discernment from You, Lord, pour it liberally upon her (him) so that all her (his) paths will be peace and life.

WEAPONS OF WARFARE

The father of the righteous will greatly rejoice, and he who begets a wise child will delight in him. Let your father and your mother be glad, and let her who bore you rejoice.
PROVERBS 23:24–25

Wisdom is the principal thing; therefore get wisdom. And in all your getting, get understanding. Exalt her, and she will promote you; she will bring you honor, when you embrace her.
PROVERBS 4:7–8

The law of the Lord is perfect, converting the soul; the testimony of the Lord is sure, making wise the simple.
PSALM 19:7

When wisdom enters your heart, and knowledge is pleasant to your soul, discretion will preserve you, understanding will keep you, to deliver you from the way of evil, from the man who speaks perverse things.
PROVERBS 2:10–12

Happy is the man who finds wisdom, and the man who gains understanding; for her proceeds are better than the profits of silver, and her gain than fine gold. She is more precious than rubies, and all the things you may desire cannot compare with her. Length of days is in her right hand, in her left hand riches and honor. Her ways are ways of pleasantness, and all her paths are peace. She is a tree of life to those who take hold of her, and happy are all who retain her.

PROVERBS 3:13–18

CHAPTER THIRTY

Growing in Faith

How many times have I heard parents of teenagers or young adults say, "My son is not motivated to do anything." "My daughter mopes around the house like she is depressed all the time." "My son is flunking out of school and doesn't seem to care." "My daughter seems lost, as if her life has no purpose." In each instance, these children are struggling with a lack of vision for their lives because they have no faith in God and His Word.

Kids without faith have a harder time in life. Kids without faith have no positive motivation, no sense of purpose, and no hope for being any different than they are. Kids without faith sit in front of the TV hour after hour, day after day, month after month. Kids without faith roam the streets looking for trouble and usually find it. Kids without faith hang around with other kids without faith, and that's the main problem with kids who are in trouble today. They don't know that Jesus died for them (Romans 5:8) and that they are God's children (John 1:12), who are loved, and have a special purpose and calling (1 Corinthians 7:22), and a bright future (1 Corinthians 2:9), and because of that they are sure winners (Romans 8:37). They don't know that "all things are possible to him who believes" (Mark 9:23), and so they don't believe there are any possibilities for their future. All they see are their own limitations and the failings and struggles of the adults around them, and so they give up.

But it's even more than that, because sensing *our* limitations doesn't necessarily mean we don't have faith. It's feeling that *God* has limitations that indicates a lack of faith. And if children don't have faith in the only thing that is secure, unchanging, and all-powerful, how can they believe in themselves and their future, which they know is insecure, unstable, and powerless?

Having raised one child so far from birth to adulthood, I've come to realize that one of the main things our children will take with them when they leave our realm of influence is their faith. If we can be sure they have strong faith in God and His Word, and the love of God in their hearts, then we can know they are set for eternity. Our prayers can play a big part in helping them achieve that.

The apostles, who were with Jesus every day, hearing Him teach and watching what He did, still had to ask of Him, "Increase our faith" (Luke 17:5). Surely *we* can ask the same for our children. "Lord, increase their faith."

The Israelites, who witnessed more miracles than we may ever see, were not allowed to enter the Promised Land because of their unbelief (Hebrews 3:19). We don't want a lack of faith to keep our children from entering into all God has promised for them. We can teach them the Word of God, which plants faith in them, and we can pray that their faith will grow.

Children who have faith have distinctly different characteristics from those who don't. They are more confident, more motivated, happier, more positive about the future, and more giving of themselves. In fact, one of the main manifestations of a person strong in faith is the ability to give—not just in terms of money or possessions, but also time, love, encouragement, and help. A person of faith is filled with God's love and looks for opportunities to share that love with others.

The Bible says, "Now abide faith, hope, love, these three; but the greatest of these is love" (1 Corinthians 13:13). In heaven, faith won't be necessary because we'll see everything. Hope won't be needed because what more could we possibly hope for? Only love will last forever, because God is love and *He* is eternal. That's why it doesn't matter what great thing we do or how much we give; if it's not done out of love, it is meaningless. "Though I bestow all my goods to feed the poor, and though I give my body to be burned, but have not love, it profits me nothing" (1 Corinthians 13:3). Everything we do out of love will last forever and the rewards are eternal.

Love is the greatest virtue. It's even greater than faith. But faith is where it begins. That's why we need to pray that as faith increases in our children, they will become God's instruments of giving. One of the reasons people don't give is that they believe there won't be enough for them if they do; another is that they don't have the love of God in their hearts for others. Pray that the principle of giving—out of love, as to the Lord, in faith, *with wisdom* and Holy Spirit guidance—be instilled in the hearts and minds of your children, because as they live accordingly, they are guaranteed to be richly blessed and fulfilled.

In any area of concern, as we begin to seriously pray in depth for our child, we often come face to face with our own need for prayer, deliverance, and restoration. How can we pray effectively for our children to be forgiving people if we are harboring unforgiveness in our own hearts? How can we pray in power for them to be repentant if we have unconfessed sin? How can we ask God to make our children faith-filled when we struggle with doubt? How can we pray for them to be givers when we have a hard time giving? I get convicted of those things too. But I don't let that stop me from praying. I go before the Lord with a humble heart, confessing what I see in myself and asking Him for help.

If, for example, you feel you don't have enough faith, confess it to God and pray the prayer at the end of this chapter with *your* name in it before you pray for your child. The Bible says that "whatever is not from faith is sin" (Romans 14:23). If we doubt, we are not obeying

God. If we have faith, we're being obedient. Doubt comes from believing that God is not all-powerful. Don't let your own lack of faith put a wall between you and God. Let it become an invitation to run to God in prayer, asking Him to increase *your* faith as well as *your child's.*

Even though this is the last of the categories for prayer focus in this book, I pray it is just the beginning for you as the Lord shows you new ways to pray for your child. Keep in mind that the power you have as a praying parent is God's power. Your prayers release that power to do God's will. It's always available, it's never in limited supply, and the only restrictions are due to lack of faith that God will answer. And even then, God's grace is such that when we don't feel we have much faith, the faith that we *do* have is like a mustard seed— enough to grow into something big.

Let's unite with other praying parents and say, "May the seeds of our faith, planted in prayer, bring forth life and grow our children into big people who follow after God's heart."

PRAYER

Lord,

You have said in Your Word that You have "dealt to each one a measure of faith" (Romans 12:3). I pray that You would take the faith You have planted in (name of child) and multiply it.

May the truth of Your Word be firmly established in his (her) heart so that faith will grow daily and navigate his (her) life. Help him (her) to trust You at all times as he (she) looks to You for truth, guidance, and transformation into Your likeness. I know that trusting in You is a choice we make. Enable him (her) to make that choice. I pray that he (she) will look to You for everything, knowing that he (she) is never without hope. May his (her) faith be the "substance of things hoped for, the evidence of things not seen" (Hebrews 11:1). I pray he (she) will have faith strong enough to lift him (her) above his circumstances and limitations and instill in him (her) the confidence of knowing that everything will work together for good (Romans 8:28).

I pray that he (she) will be so strong in faith that his (her) relationship with You supersedes all else in his (her) life—even my influence as a parent. In other words, may he (she) have a relationship with You, Lord, that is truly his (her) own—not an extension of mine or anyone else's. I want the comfort of knowing that when I'm no longer on this earth, his (her) faith will be strong enough to keep him (her) "steadfast, immovable, always abounding in the work of the Lord" (1 Corinthians 15:58).

As he (she) walks in faith, may he (she) have Your heart of love that overflows to others, a heart that is willing to give of self and possessions according to Your leading. May he (she) see that giving out of love is actually giving *back* to You in faith and that he (she) will never lose anything by doing so. I pray that he (she) will take the "shield

of faith" in order to "quench all the fiery darts of
the wicked one" (Ephesians 6:16), and thereby be
able to stand strong in faith and say, "I thank
Christ Jesus our Lord who has enabled me,
because He counted me faithful" (1 Timothy
1:12). In Jesus' name, I pray all of these things.

WEAPONS OF WARFARE

Without faith it is impossible to please Him, for he who
comes to God must believe that He is, and that He is a
rewarder of those who diligently seek Him.
HEBREWS 11:6

Therefore I say to you, whatever things you ask
when you pray, believe that you receive them,
and you will have them.
MARK 11:24

If you have faith as a mustard seed, you will say to
this mountain, "Move from here to there," and it will
move; and nothing will be impossible for you.
MATTHEW 17:20

But let him ask in faith, with no doubting, for he who
doubts is like a wave of the sea driven and tossed by
the wind. For let not that man suppose that he will
receive anything from the Lord; he is a double-minded
man, unstable in all his ways.
JAMES 1:6–8

And let us not grow weary while doing good, for in due season we shall reap if we do not lose heart. Therefore, as we have opportunity, let us do good to all, especially to those who are of the household of faith.

GALATIANS 6:9–10

APPENDIX

Praying Together
with Other Parents

After experimenting with a number of ways to organize an intercessory prayer time for children, I found a format that works well. First of all, each prayer gathering has to be limited to praying for no more than twelve children at a time, because it takes twenty to thirty minutes per child to share concerns and requests and adequately pray for them. Even with only twelve children, that means six hours of praying. This is quite a sacrifice of time and commitment as a parent, not to mention how much it pushes the limits of patience for the children. That's why we only do it once or twice a year—usually on a Saturday or holiday.

The way we organize it is to start praying at 2:00 P.M., take a dinner break from 5:00 to 5:30 P.M. and then pray from 5:30 to 8:30 P.M. Sometimes everyone brings food to share; sometimes we order food to be delivered. We hire teenagers to keep the younger children entertained and cared for in a separate room while the adults pray in private.

We have found it doesn't work well to pray for all the children in a family one after the other, because often that family feels they're done at that point and might as well go home. It's also not good for people to drop in to be prayed for and then leave—or even worse, drop the child off to be prayed for and then come back and pick him (her) up. The only time we were happy to do that was in the case of a single parent who worked and couldn't arrange it otherwise. For the most part, this prayer time must be a commitment of *all* the parents to *all* the children for *all* the time it takes. Let people know in advance what's expected of them in this regard so they can decide whether they are able to make the commitment.

When we begin, we draw the names of each family to see in what order we will proceed. Then we pray in that order, one at a time, for the firstborn of every family. When we've finished with them, we pray for the second born, then the third born, and so on.

We always begin the prayer time without the child present so the parents can give their requests and concerns and we can pray for any sensitive issues which they don't want the child to hear. Then we invite the child into the room to share his (her) own specific requests. As we pray for those requests, we also pray for the child's health, safety, protection, guidance, development of gifts and talents, and possibly discreet mention of the previously stated concern of the parent.

For example, one parent expressed concern over the bad influence of certain friends in the child's life. When we prayed *without* the child, we interceded in great detail about the specific friends. When we prayed *with* the child, we prayed for the child to have discernment to seek out godly friends and resist ungodly associates. Discretion is the key here so that the child never feels betrayed or judged, but only loved.

The families we have prayed with over the years still talk about the powerful impact of our times together and the many answers to prayer that came about as a result. The children also enjoyed these prayer sessions because it made them feel cared for and special. There were even instances where parents came to have the group pray for an adult child living away from home, and they also later testified to the positive effect of those prayers.

Who knows how many lives have been—or can be—saved in one way or another just because praying parents join together? Don't be hesitant to organize a praying parent group in your area. The need is great. If you organize it, the people will come.

Other Good
Harvest House Reading

STORMIE
by *Stormie Omartian*

The childhood of singer/songwriter Stormie Omartian, marred by physical and emotional abuse, led into teen and adult years filled with tragedy. Searching for an end to the inner turmoil which constantly confronted her, Stormie found herself on the verge of suicide. In this poignant story there is help and hope for anyone who doubts the value of his or her own life. It gloriously reveals a God who can bring life out of death if we are willing to surrender to His ways.

GREATER HEALTH GOD'S WAY
by *Stormie Omartian*

Providing a creative, practical approach to developing a person's mind, body, and spirit. Omartian offers a successful alternative to traditional diet and exercise programs.

THE POWER OF A PRAYING WIFE
by *Stormie Omartian*

Wives will learn how God created the marriage relationship to be a healthy, rich, fulfilling, and fruitful part of His plan. Women trapped in an empty or rocky marriage can discover lifechanging breakthroughs as they learn how to effectively pray for their husbands. And those in a solid and happy marriage can strengthen their relationship and gain an even deeper intimacy.